Published by Ockley Books Limited

First published December 2021

ISBN 978-1-910906-25-5

Layout & design by GD Associates,
front cover by Michael Kinlan

Printed & bound by:
Biddles Printing, King's Lynn

Soul

Beyond the Athlete

OCKLEY BOOKS
.com

For those who need it and
those who can make great
change with it.

Contents

Prologue

Love dares you to care for the people on the edge of the night

And love dares you to change our way of caring about ourselves

This is our last dance

This is ourselves

(David Bowie / John Deacon / Brian May / Freddie Mercury / Roger Taylor)

After I wrote *Mensch* I was left with one question: what does modern, professional sport do for the person behind the player? It's clear how much of an effect sports teams and their performance can have on a community and a fan base, but inside the world of professional sport what happens to the human being in the game?

Highlighting the need to look after people in football was one of the key factors behind writing *Mensch*, and why the title is the German word for person. But in the context of a collection of stories about what it takes to be a great coach it remained one attribute aiding the possibility of success. I wanted to make it the sole focus, learn more and look outside of Germany's borders.

How much were clubs, leagues and organisations really doing (or not doing) to help develop the person as much as the player? I wanted to look at the details of duty of care, player care and well-being. Was enough being done to develop young men and women beyond how many opponents they can beat and how fast they can run? This was about education, but also a kind of human development existing beyond a classroom.

Looking after the person outside of their sporting performance should not be considered an approach required only to tick a box. This is as much a responsibility as it is a moral choice. The lives of athletes and coaches are not designed solely to deliver entertainment once or twice a week.

I spoke to coaches, psychologists and athletes across Europe, North America and Australia about what human development means to them. Almost all of them were fighting against structures and the age-old sentiment of 'we've always done it this way' to facilitate a more human-focussed environment.

I was fortunate to hear how different approaches to youth football could make all the difference to the child's life later on, how changing the philosophy of a club to be people-focussed was possible, why the support and growth of coaches mustn't be lost in this discussion, and how the culture of a country can have a telling impact on young people's lives and their view of sport.

Understanding that people are at the heart of every pursuit is bigger than football. That is one of the reasons I was even more passionate about sharing this work than *Mensch*. As the world's population expands and competition increases to the point where we are more often pitted against one another rather than encouraged to help one another, understanding our own life is hard. It is a struggle to realise our own purpose, realise our own dreams. At a time when the clouds are gathering, both literally and figuratively, we mustn't forget that our friends, colleagues, employees, neighbours, teammates and family are all doing their best to balance their lives. It sounds so simple, almost ridiculous, but how often do we truly consider that in others?

Soul is a piece of work about why, whatever we do, we must remember people. Nurturing, helping, listening to and supporting the person will allow for growth that helps the professional, the employee, the player and the game. However complex and political the environment, the club or the situation, a philosophical change to put people at the heart of what you do can change everything for the better of the organisation, the individuals and ultimately the world.

With football, indeed much of sport, becoming an increasingly ruthless world of entertainment, physical strength, financial gain and the ego, our soul is often forgotten. It is time to start a conversation to change that, to put our soul back in the foreground. It is time to look beyond the athlete. The words of Queen & David Bowie's 1981 hit single 'Under Pressure' are at the beginning of this prologue because it is time to change how we care about ourselves and one another. Perhaps this is not our last chance to consider how we love, but rather our last chance to look after the soul.

1

Denmark

Does professional sport care for people? It's a simple question and on the face of it the answer is yes. Major sports such as football, basketball, American football and tennis offer people with the requisite sporting skill and physical ability an opportunity to make playing sport a career that is both fulfilling and financially beneficial. It gives people the chance to understand and develop their body, play and master a sport they enjoy every day and accrue wealth that will change the lives of their families for generations. On the face of it, there doesn't appear to be a downside.

But what about who they really are off the field? Does sport care about that? And if so what is being done about it? The perception that athletes live in another world is common but technically untrue. They live in the same world albeit generally with greater means at their disposal. With that comes unrealistic expectation from thousands of people, plus the perils of fame and excessive finance, all within a ruthlessly small window in which they must perform or be replaced.

In recent years, non-sporting support for athletes has grown. Established sports psychology intervention models aim at providing solutions to behavioural, emotional and cognitive problems in everyone at an organisation. Beyond sports psychologists though, there are also coaches spreading across a range of fields - mental, performance, life, cognitive - all aimed at improving the ability to perform.

Again though, we return to the person. Not in the context of what they provide as an athlete or a performer, but what they feel, think, say, depict and stand for. Furthermore, does sport even have to consider the personal development of an athlete given all of the professional development it is already invested in?

In research around human development and looking after the person, I was often confronted with the simple fact that professional sport has no place for it. High-level professional sport is solely about delivering top-level performances week in, week out so as to win. Unless your approach can help bring that victory closer then there is no place for you.

My problem with that is sport cannot just be about winning. During the course of a playing or coaching career the desire to win, to achieve something others have not, to be the best is undoubtedly a factor. However, when the majority of players and coaches look back on their careers I believe it is not so much the winning they remember but rather the people they played with and the places they played in.

Teams stand for something, and even though that has been marketed to the detriment of the original values it is clear that choosing to play for a team represents a choice to represent a certain set of values and a certain community. Players have also always stood for something but in recent years, with the arrival of social media and increased advertising opportunities, players have become as much of a brand as clubs. Inevitably, a lot of those choices are driven by finance. But players developing their own brand, along with the dramatic rise in video game formats that allow for the self assembly of top players in one team, plus fantasy sports, have led to an increase in people supporting players rather than teams. Some are probably supported because they win, but most of them are supported because of their brand.

The video game influence is not to be underestimated. Not only is it a billion-dollar industry, but it has impacted the modern perception of modern games.

That is enhanced by Game Transfer Phenomena (GTP), a psychological state that occurs when players integrate elements of video game playing into real life by way of thoughts, sensations, and actions.

Considering that players are regularly photographed with ratings in the virtual world, the increasing realism and popularity of sports gaming, the social impact on language and interaction that the games have, it's hardly surprising that the lines between real and virtual worlds might blur. And this affects human development in a subtle and simple way. If our perception of human beings is influenced by similar-looking pixels in a virtual world then we are not far away from asking why player x doesn't cross the ball better when we know their crossing is rated at 92 in the game. We are not far away from forgetting, if just for a moment, that these two worlds are indeed worlds apart.

Indeed, those worlds collided during the 2021 NFL Draft. When players were selected and walked onto the stage, the usual player statistics were shown on the screen but this year they were accompanied by a "Draft Score." This score, delivered by Next Gen Stats (powered by Amazon Web Services), gave player ratings out of 100 just like in the popular American football video game *Madden* for traits such as athleticism, production and overall. The assessment of real players being shown to everyone watching the draft was similar if not identical to those used in their virtual representations in the sport's most popular video game. In that moment it was hard to tell who was influencing who, the person or the pixel.

In order for human development to take root, decision makers in boardrooms will have to be convinced. There are plenty of players, coaches and teams who have shown that with an holistic approach, teams can win and demonstrate the right kind of values. However, there are many who have shown that with little consideration for the human perspective, great sporting success can be achieved.

Renowned professor and sports psychologist Dr Wade Gilbert told me that "people are like water, they take the shape they are put in." In sport, that shape is always performance, but I wondered what would happen if the shape was the person and not performance. That's why I boarded a train to Copenhagen.

I first spoke to Frederik Bløndal the day he lost his job. Bløndal spoke to me over the phone after being dismissed from his role at a grassroots club because he wanted more focus to be put on the development of the kids. Bløndal wanted to stop biased early selection that comes from focussing on physical development, and create a fair system that prevents relative age effect and focusses on the development of all kids. Relative age affect, RAE for short, is the development, practice time and physical advantages that an autumn birth date, immediately after the academic year cut-off (September 1st) brings. A few weeks after our phone conversation, I was sat in his Bløndal's dining room with his wonderful family talking about Denmark, relative age effect and the people he knows doing their best to establish human development in the country.

Frederik's main job however, is as Denmark's U16 physiotherapist and just a day after our meeting in the Danish capital he was flying to England to take part in a competition. Perhaps tellingly, he told me how boring these trips can sometimes be for players. There's a lot of waiting and resting. Although the sacrifice many young players make has come to light more recently, this is a further reminder that the football life reflected on television screens or on social media is often some distance from the reality.

At one point we get to talking about human development in

football and how complex it is. The question arises: are we perhaps just happier not knowing about the complexities? There's no denying that it is easier to rely on the plans of a session and the numbers of analytics. There's also a great deal of value to be found in them. But looking the other way when it comes to human development doesn't mean that it no longer exists. At a time when awareness about mental health is finally growing, the virtual world poses even greater opportunity and risk, and the planet is changing, we must acknowledge how we feel. What we think and why we act certain ways is important. We must also try to acknowledge all of the above in others.

If we do not, then we return to a place where the player is more important the person, where what they offer now is more important than the ability to nurture. There is perhaps no better example of this issue than relative age effect.

Children born in the last three months of the year are being neglected because the kids born in the first three months of the year are physically bigger. That size can make all the difference at younger ages, but it brings with it a two-pronged threat. Firstly, the reliance on those bigger kids means that too often when they get older their development has stalled. Their size gave them advantages, which meant they were less likely to be developed, but when their size no longer became an advantage they often had little else to fall back on. Secondly, those kids born at the end of the year are regularly forgotten or disregarded because they're small. Ironically, this early adversity can be an advantage as they're determined to show that they are good enough. Most of the best players in the world are, after all, small.

Danish is a funny language. In many ways it sounds like German after three beers. Despite being intrigued by the rhythms of the words, I was relieved to be able to speak to Piotr Haren in a more familiar language. Haren is a director of Lyngby's academy and coaching. Lyngby, a club recently famous for being saved from death by friends and former members, is based in a northern suburb of Copenhagen. The club has history in the UEFA Cup, as well as the European Cup, but life in the Danish league has been a bit tougher.

They are famous for their youth development though, and four of the Danish squad at the end of 2019 were players who started their careers at Lyngby. Bundesliga talents Yussuf Poulsen and Jacob Bruun Larsen started at the club, as did Lasse Schöne,

Christian Gytkjær and Dennis Rommedahl. Their title haul might be modest, but the number of players that have gone on to enjoy successful careers after starting at Lyngby is worth boasting about.

Haren, a former Superliga player and school teacher, is as humble as they come though. "The worst thing to happen to Denmark was winning the 1992 Euros," Haren tells me as we sit in a small inside café in Copenhagen. "We played in a negative way. And this from a team that used to be called the Scandinavian Brazil!"

These words are familiar to the ones I heard from Helmut Groß in *Mensch*, when the legendary coach explained to me that Germany's problem was winning the 1990 World Cup without a plan. Success can blind many to the problems in or with the system, and Haren feels that success has contributed to Denmark's problems since.

Some of the core issues facing football in Denmark include a mindset issue that sees some in the country believe that Denmark is the centre of the world. The Danes are certainly not the only country in the world with this issue, but it serves as a reminder that one of the greatest inhibitors to change is a refusal to look outside of what we know. We need more humility. As David Brooks writes in *The Road to Character*, *"humility is the awareness that there's a lot you don't know and that a lot of what you think you know is distorted or wrong."* Acceptance of that is not only absolutely okay, but it also leads to increased wisdom.

Haren's list, sadly, goes on. Pitch quality is a major problem in Denmark, there is far too much administrative work demanded from coaching, general attendance is low, some coaches and players don't have a handle on their emotions, the quality of the SuperLiga is not high, and too many young coaches are getting jobs they're not qualified for in academies because of a lack of money.

It might be hard to believe in a country like Denmark, but salaries in football are a relative problem. Haren tells me the average annual salary is around €120,000. Further research via the Economic Research Institute suggests it is closer to €290,000. Either way, in the context of football, it remains modest.

Haren remembers visiting Cambridge United once and having the dramatic realisation that the salaries at the League Two team matched the bottom clubs in Denmark's top-flight. To be involved in Danish football, you have to really love it because there are plenty of other jobs in the country that pay better. It is worth acknowledging the benefit of this on wider society and the impact it has on the balance of the sport.

However, it does mean that most clubs struggle to survive. FC Copenhagen, aided by Champions League money, are the exception as they have an advantage over every other club in the country. This can breed innovation, but it's not easy, especially not in an environment that believes in the application of old routines and struggles to look beyond its own perspective.

Another issue is that footballers don't have room to learn a trade. For those kids who want to take a step towards professional football, an academy education is a must. While education is never something to be sacrificed, this seems unnecessarily rigid. There appears no obvious reason why other pathways are limited for a group of young people striving for a dream that very few can realistically realise. Denying them a chance to develop a trade, something they may like and something that is arguably of underestimated importance today, doesn't appear to be in unison with recognising the human development of individuals.

Denmark does have greater freedom than other countries though. Many clubs in Denmark do not have a hierarchal issue. There is far more freedom at clubs like Lyngby to be able to make collective decisions. Clearly, flat hierarchies bring their own problems with them, but in such contexts they can have huge advantages.

One of those is collective input and responsibility. For example, all of the coaches at Lyngby decide the curriculum, and they have reflected their desire to figure it out by working together in their environment. Rather than being given all of the information, young players and coaches are encouraged to figure it out themselves. "We need more eureka moments. Figuring it out yourself is of far greater value than just being told," Haren tells me.

The combination of the lack of funds and being the fourth club in Copenhagen (FC Copenhagen, Brondby, Nordsjælland) has forced Lyngby to think differently. In a necessary decision to survive, the club only recruit locally and have focussed on the smaller players. This is not an unusual approach, as Haren tells me. Another top-flight side, Silkeborg IF, have built a model of finding young players who are left-footed. Football finds a way.

While there are doubtless problems with this approach too, Haren uses it to demonstrate one of the major flaws with the top-down hierarchy often at play in football. At a recent conference, Haren saw a presentation by Wolverhampton Wanderers' scouting department. They revealed that they deliver 2,000 player reports a month. This figure is astronomical, and prompted a moment of hilarity for the Danish coaches. Not only would you need a veritable army to deliver such a number every month, but there's also the cost. While casting the net wide has its advantages, this seems unrealistically broad, almost as if there is no clear plan whatsoever. Clearly, there is also room to criticise some of the Danish clubs for their narrow search parameters, but that would be to miss that theirs is done out of necessity. Too much money can lead to not only too much information, but plenty of irrelevant information. Most importantly, even if these reports include any form of human assessment, how accurate could they possibly be if they are just one report in a group of 2,000?

Haren believes the key is to find an approach that fits the player, one that includes the development of life skills and local culture. Only then will we be able to understand one another. Lyngby's situation has helped them carve a niche for themselves. They made the most of their adversity and in the academy have developed an environment where all coaches get to have a say and where players are encouraged to fit the pieces together themselves rather than follow instructions. This approach is reflected in the club's modest surroundings, both in terms of their stadium and their academy.

This is in stark contrast to FC Nordsjælland, a club some consider ahead of the curve when it comes to development, particularly the development of social skills. Some believe a handful of the U16s could probably play in the first team, but that too many of the players struggle when they leave. The club situated in the town of Farum on the country's largest island, Zealand, felt very different to the Lyngby that Haren had described.

After a short walk from the station, The Right To Dream Park looms. The 10,300-seater stadium was built in 2000 and was the first stadium in Denmark's top flight to have artificial turf. It looks clean and new, and might even appear shiny were it not for the cold wind blowing in.

Inside, I meet Tom Vernon, the chairman of FC Nordsjælland and the founder of Right to Dream. His office overlooks the pitch, but feels different to the stereotypical chairman's office. This one feels lighter. It is evident Vernon cares about his choice of words. It speaks highly of him too that he takes a genuine interest, despite the fact it isn't long until he has a meeting and his phone is constantly buzzing. Even in our short encounter, I understood what Vernon was doing was impressive. It was clear he was someone who had the business acumen to make his attempts to create new and flexible structures of personal development possible. He had been there and done it before marketing videos on it were necessary. As such, it was unsurprising to hear him a couple of years later on the *Football Ramble* podcast talk diligently about subjects such as acknowledging the baggage that comes with being a white Englishman in Ghana and the importance of not inserting cultures into development structures in sport or society.

In 2003, Farum BK, despite finishing third in the SuperLiga as a newly-promoted side, were close to bankruptcy after financial irregularities from their chairman. Local businessman Allan Pedersen bought the club and changed the name to FC Nordsjælland, as well as setting up a network of local teams in the hope of finding young talent in the area. In 2012, the club won the Danish title, beating favourites Copenhagen. That success landed them a spot in the 2012-13 Champions League group stages and although they finished bottom of Group E, the financial realm of possibility for the club had changed.

In January 2016, Tom Vernon, former Manchester United scout and founder of Ghana's largest football academy Right to Dream, bought FC Nordsjælland with a group of investors. Right to Dream opened in 2009 and integrates elite football coaching, schooling and character development for boys and girls looking to excel in sport or other fields. The Nordsjælland academy opens a pathway for people to make their way into European football or life beyond the field. Pivotally, the connection also enables young local Danish kids to visit Ghana, play football and meet the people. Right to Dream also regularly wins three to five student-athlete scholarships a year at some of the best colleges in America.

Right to Dream hasn't stopped there either. In 2020, they

brought in former Head of People and Team Development at the English FA, Dr Pippa Grange, to become their Head of Culture, with a clear focus on people and purpose across the club. A year later, Right to Dream announced they would be building an academy for boys and girls in Egypt. It feels like this is very much the beginning for Vernon and his team.

The club is clearly doing things differently, and they state that their goal is to build a team made up entirely of academy players. This is about opportunity and the development of human beings. Opportunity is one of the great separators. The opportunity to work, learn, develop, live, progress, speak; reaching thousands. There are endless people in the world with the will to do more, help more, become more, but often it is the opportunity that lies beyond them.

Nordsjælland are giving those at their club that chance. They believe the development of character in those early years is pivotal to forming the whole person later on.

That's why the club have designated mental and character coaches.

And in the lobby of the club's stadium having just watched the U19s play a friendly against Brondby's U19s, I met with mental coach for the U15-U19s as well as the first team, Carsten Hvid Larsen. The associate professor with a PhD is also a sports psychologist and a co-author of a book called *Mindfulness and Acceptance in Sport - How to help athletes perform and thrive under pressure*. Larsen provides support for youth teams and the first team, both for players and coaches, by attending training sessions, making observations and giving feedback. Once a month he offers a workshop to the coaches to review their work. At the time of our meeting they were discussing stress recovery and pressure.

Alongside the obvious sporting development that comes with being at a professional football club, Nordsjælland is also interested in nurturing more personable skills such as attitude, purpose and character. This is undoubtedly an unusual approach to football, but for Larsen it is simply a product of the environment.

"The system has to be in the same place, otherwise sports psychology is treated as different or new and put in the classroom, and there is no transfer [from classroom to pitch]," Larsen tells me.

This transfer is key. Much of the work done in a classroom environment, whether to educate tactical, technical or emotional understanding, can be problematic as the setting comes with a number of triggers. For many, school was not a happy or encouraging place, and the classroom itself comes with connections to tests. Taking the learning done here and transferring it onto the pitch and life is pivotal to the success of the human development at the club. Otherwise, behavioural change becomes another subject on the schedule rather than an active, on-going development.

Too often, the work that Larsen does has been seen as the footnote or the last box to tick in football. Larsen's holistic ecological approach to sports psychology is an attempt to change the culture. "You have to slowly massage the change in," Larsen says with a smile.

In individual sports, the development of the mind is quite normal. For some reason, in team sports it is often neglected. Perhaps we consider the collective capable of making up for our own individual difficulties, but this is a mistake. "The collective is impacted by the individual. We need to focus on that," Larsen tells me. The club and Larsen are both keen on developing the idea of mindfulness. Without this, consideration of others, general openness and the formation of a team through individual understanding is much harder. The word is also linked to purpose, and the two words probably form the bedrock of the work being done to help human beings at the club.

It's clear that Nordsjælland are doing something different, and Larsen is grateful to be in this environment. "It is unusual to have no egos in the coaching staff, but that is because we are all pulling on the same rope," Larsen says. This is because of the club's philosophy, which is quite clearly focussed on developing young people.

Changing the culture to allow for greater focus on Larsen's holistic ecological approach to sports psychology has not gone unnoticed. Both Wolfsburg and Manchester United are apparently interested in it, and I noticed a group of RB Leipzig coaches wandering around during my visit. Whether or not they're able to generate the same approach given the varying culture at each club is questionable, but there are clearly ideas here that can be and should be considered for wider use.

Nordsjælland are keen on that too, which immediately

attracts suspicion in a sport where people are desperate to get ahead and keep secrets. It is their desire to share their approach that shows their willingness to help generate widespread change, rather than just in one small area of Denmark and Ghana. One of the most unusual aspects of the club's approach is the character development guidance the club has, and later on I sat down with the club's head of character development and player education, Will Orben, to understand it better.

Orben explains to me that the club delivers character development lessons once a week from U10s all the way up to the first team. "Keeping seven key character traits in mind, the teams move through four, seven session units over the course of the season covering age-specific topics."

Most of those sessions will be done with Will, one will be one-on-one, two to three will be done by coaches. It takes six years to go through every area of focus.

"It's so important that it's not just football we focus on. We owe it to each player's identity," Orben tells me. The club has done a great job creating a varied curriculum for character development rather than just coming into a room to talk about abstract topics and why they're important. More pivotally though, they have recognised the value in not explicitly outlining a training plan for this approach. Developing greater understanding around transition, resilience, purpose and integrity, means learning through doing most of the time. Plenty of information is discussed and activities are included so as to avoid it feeling like a classroom setting. After that, it's simple. "We trust them to make good decisions," Orben tells me.

Later that day, I sit in on the final few minutes of an U13 session run by the club's other character development coach, and former player, James C. Nortey. The session was focussed around the idea of identifying an area to improve team culture. Nortey, just 28, is a natural in this environment. He recognises that such phrasing might be too grand for an U13 group and so brings it back to the simple question: what does the team need?

Decisively though, he also embodies character development. This process of helping others and understanding his knowledge can be used to help others is something Nortey has literally put into action. Towards the end of 2019, he set out to use boxing as a vehicle to teach and develop people in his hometown of Bokum, a small community on the coast of Accra in Ghana. It is clear that he understands the meaning of the words and the sentiments he is teaching. Furthermore, his story is one that many young kids in the local area will never have heard before. Growing up around different cultures can only be of benefit to their human development.

The U13s are sat in a semicircle around a big screen with plenty of questions: what can you contribute, what difference can you make, what did you learn? These are questions the children are required to answer by the end of three weeks, having been able to assess what the team needs in action. With the culture of the club clear from the start, the onus is on the kids to ask questions and find their own way to develop.

Nortey tells me afterwards that the U13-U16 are the most engaged, with the difference between the girls and the boys illuminating. When they did a session on ambitions, the girls' group had broader thoughts about their future including love and a family while the boys all focussed on becoming a professional footballer. On the one hand, this is further proof that girls mature faster than boys. It may also be damning evidence to suggest that still far too many young girls with aspirations to become professional footballers don't think it's a possibility and so are already, even at younger ages, thinking of other plans in life.

The U17 to U19 group is apparently and yet unsurprisingly harder to work with because professional sport looms large on the horizon. Herein lies perhaps the biggest problem. The work being done at younger age groups appears invaluable. Exposure to different countries and cultures, a curriculum of character development delivered through a mix of classroom and activity-based lessons, a club philosophy that nurtures those traits through relationship building and the maintaining of an environment of trust and growth - it's a great structure for human development. However, the moment the football becomes tangible, character development turns into a subject on the schedule again. So deep are the lures of the professional game that it's hard to maintain a level of focus around personal growth, and yet it is exactly at that time that character development must be maintained. The foundation built for so many at Nordsjælland stands them in excellent stead to succeed, but it is at those later teenager years that that foundation must be built upon. Like a house is never finished, neither is a person. Your learning is never complete and at a time of increased media attention the circle of influence will grow and figures will be thrown around that are both tempting and foreign. Looking after the human is key.

"The contract on the table has to be matched by care," Orben says, diligently. Money is nothing more than numbers. Some have more than others, but we all have minds and thoughts open to the same pain, love, joy and fear. Having that not just cared for but also exposed to a learning environment is hugely important for so many obvious reasons, but also because of the message it sends if we don't, namely that your only value here is your professional ability.

It is clear that everything here is connected. The style of play - expansive, open, team-orientated - is linked to the club's character development. Nordsjælland want to play football in the same way they want to help people grow into more open, socially conscious and empathetic humans. The first team is heavily connected to the academy, making movement fluid throughout the system. At the time of my visit Nordsjælland were looking to improve mentorship programmes between the U19s and the U14s. The club is also helping relationship building and understanding by getting players to speak to people throughout the club, from kit men to staff members working in finance. As the virtual world increases in importance and strength, such face-to-face interactions help sharpen both social skills and the lines between the two worlds. It is one thing to message someone on your phone; it is quite another to talk to them in person. The club are consciously looking to do more of the latter because they know reducing isolation - which messes with character and stability - is one of the best ways to help people learn about who they are. On International Women's Day, not only did the successful women's team spend time with the men's team, but the names on the back of the jerseys of the first team were changed to the names of inspirational women. Having spent time learning about inspirational women around the world, the players were also able to select their role models themselves, explaining their reasons on social media. Some may consider the move nothing more than a marketing gimmick, but given that the players spent time learning about inspirational women and made a conscious choice who they wanted to represent suggests that the club's increased profile was a byproduct of the move rather than the aim.

"The changing of the culture starts at a younger age. You can't just slap it on," Orben tells me.

The implementation of character development through every stage of the academy suggests that Nordsjælland's approach is progressive rather than short term. What's also key is the focus being on learning that isn't just classroom-based. In the overall environment ego amongst coaches does not play a role, relationships with people throughout the club are encouraged, and there is a regular exchange between countries, cultures and genders. Nordsjælland really are a club that has human development at its centre.

Simply taking the time to do character work is a bold move. Many schools and places embrace character development but not as an explicit topic. At Nordsjælland, character building is for everyone, an active representation of the club's philosophy.

Over 650 kilometres away, the academy of another club is trying to create human development purely through the environment it creates, one that takes into consideration the culture of the local area and is built from connections between people. There is no classroom character development here. It's all done outside.

2

Sweden

If you have enough time, and it is a big if, it is possible to get almost anywhere in Europe on a train. The trip across the bridge from Hamburg to Denmark was stirring, but racing past the lakes and mossy trees of rural Sweden brought an almost paradoxical level of calm. I felt as though I was returning to some form of the natural world, but was hurtling along in an enormous machine of metal.

Having managed to go north for long enough, my next stop was top-flight Swedish club AIK. They believe that systemic change is required to foster human development. The club's academy and home ground are in Solna, a municipality of Stockholm that has more workplaces than residents. Fitting in with this busy area of work is AIK's stadium, the Friends Arena. It is a large, multi-event venue that is also Sweden's national stadium and is named after Friends, an organisation dedicated to preventing bullying in schools and sports. It is connected to the 'Mall of Scandinavia', the largest shopping centre in the country. Some at the club call it 'The Museum of America'.

The club's academy couldn't have been more different. Perhaps while not intentional, it perfectly reflects the club's values-based approach. Around a junction near the Solna underground station sit the pitches and academy building. The changing rooms and gym are built inside an old bomb shelter, stripping the facility back to the bare bones and adding a genuine feel to the place. Should such the shelter be needed for its original purpose again, the club has 48 hours to transform humble academy surroundings back to a place of safety.

There is nothing extra, no show. It feels like a place of work, there are no frills here. It provides the opportunity to focus on the work at hand as well as people. Around the corner there is plenty of buying happening, with people encouraged to purchase a number of items. It is somewhat poetic that just around the corner, AIK's academy is doing the opposite. The club is creating an atmosphere that breaks free of many academy approaches by not entering the commodity market. Here players are people not things. The buy and sell culture has been replaced by one of care and camaraderie.

Jürgen Klopp's decision to keep Borussia Dortmund's changing rooms simple like a lower league team was because of his belief that the changing room was a place of work and there was no need for distraction or excess. AIK's academy has taken a similar step. In a space of higher learning where special skills are taught, there is a distinct effort here to make sure young people are not afforded every luxury. Too much too soon is a hard place to come back from. This is what an academy should feel like.

I was first drawn to the club because of James Vaughan, a former futsal player for New Zealand who is now head of player development for U13-U19s at AIK. Vaughan, who has a PhD in sports coaching and creativity in football, was also one of many academics either at the club or spending time in and around the club. Many are interested in the structural changes the club have made and how they allow for new ways of working to grow. While undoubtedly a surprise to see so many academics working at a football club in a somewhat philosophical field, it felt like the innovation the club was making was directly linked to the cumulation of many smart minds in the same place. It was also worth noting that most of the academics I met were also high-level coaches and educators, creating a seemingly formidable source of burgeoning football minds.

Vaughan was researching the intriguing topic of how culture impacts football and creativity. The impact of culture on a club can in turn have intriguing impacts on how and whether a club decides to develop humans. In an article for the *Player Development Project*, an online coaching resource entitled 'Who We Are Is How We Play', Vaughan wrote about cultural conditioning.

"Our early experiences, shaped by people and places, impact not only our long-term player development, but also the way we live our lives. If we can understand a player's cultural conditioning we can begin to understand their mindset, giving insight into how they make choices and why they see the world the way they do – but as coaches we must seek to understand before being understood."

Analysis of this early experience need not be limited to just the sports we played, but rather the people we met, the places we visited, the activities we loved to do.

AIK academy's decision - the academy is separate from the corporate side of the club that owns 49 percent - to prioritise a values-based approach rather than an economic one is certainly a sign of recognising the need for human development. In his thesis, Vaughan explains how those values end up on the pitch.

Dennis Hörtin, head of children's and youth operations and research and development at the club, believes that creating a culture built around values and not money is key. Money will come - there's enough in football - but taking an approach that is more human-focussed allows for greater consideration of the many. AIK have created an environment where players making the professional level are a byproduct not the goal.

In doing so, what the club has done is create opportunities for relationships to be formed, and for children to ask questions about the development they're undergoing rather than simply undergo it themselves. Making the conscious decision to provide more autonomy should lead to more human development - and it all starts with one radical change the club made three years ago.

Not long after the club sold Alexander Isak to Borussia Dortmund they took a drastic change to their approach. The club decided to delay selection until the age of 13. One UEFA A or B qualified head coach was placed in charge of each age group aged 8-12 to actively engage with and support players, parent coaches, coaches and parents. One of the best parent coaches was a former ultra, and someone who totally agreed with the radical approach.

Speaking to Swedish sports newspaper *Sportbladet*, Hörtin explained the importance of having one staff member of every age acting as a support for parent coaches and parents. *"The coaches and parents see this person in their everyday lives and understand that there is someone who cares. Suddenly, the commitment increases. We have had external coaches from the age of ten before but now we are up to 12 and soon 13. You can do this if you think in a different way and build social relationships in the club."*

Building these connections is at the heart of everything the club wants to do. The decision to move selection to 13 was made following a strategy built around the aforementioned trio of principles. The player then gets to decide their own path, including training opportunities, based on their degree of internal motivation. They can either decide to specialise and go all in on football, training four times a week and playing on the weekend or they can choose to generalise and train at least twice a week, but without football being the main sport. Football may stay the main sport, but they might just want to play with friends more often. Those who do specialise and join the academy, and the connected school, are primarily kids from the area. Pivotally, kids can make this decision each calendar year until they reach 18 years old.

"As many as possible, as long as possible, in the best possible environment" is the motto AIK are trying to pursue. They are conscious of the collective and are not only focussing on the one or two players that might make the transition to the first team.

One of the figures in this development is Mark O'Sullivan, the club's player and coach development mentor. O'Sullivan's greatest analogy refers to current generic linear development models, typical of many modern academies and elite-level youth sport in general. While speaking at an event, O'Sullivan asked for a bag of eggs - one hard-boiled. To make his point, he threw the bag on the floor and then picked up the one unbroken egg and said: "The system works!"

O'Sullivan has a deeper, perhaps darker, version of this theory, one he says was inspired by something similar he heard John Kiely, a senior lecturer in elite performance, once say. "Talent is the graveyard of evidence. Nobody sees the dead bodies."

Who defines talent? Even the dictionary definition of the word, "a special often athletic, creative, or artistic aptitude", remains vague.

The word has become an aura, an intangible feeling thrown around by those who possess a mystical level of understanding. In many ways it has blinded us from the many because the nurturing of a talented player, regardless of what happens to others, is too common.

Perhaps "bodies" is too harsh, although the reasons for using it are understandable. "Shadows" may be an even more appropriate word given that they are both present and yet not really there - much like the perception around the players who don't make the transition to the first team. The win has become more important, the destination more of a draw than the journey. The path to developing young footballers may often be paved with good and bad intentions. Not only does it too often lead to shattered dreams, but it is lined with the shadows of those who didn't make it.

A non-linear pedagogy is the way AIK are trying to counter this in session design. O'Sullivan explains how the interactions of three constraints - Individual, Environment and Task - form the foundation of helping coaches develop along with understanding of the learner and the learning process. Individual includes the physical and mental constraints a player might have, whereas Environment relates to the weather and the facilities but also to their family, peers, and life growing up. Task is about the exercise in front of them - how many players, the size of the pitch, their instructions to perform the task.

Indeed, such is the extent of the work being done by O'Sullivan and his peers that after he and four others published a paper on "Conceptualising physical literacy within an ecological dynamics framework" in *Quest*, the leading journal for work on kinesiology, the Swedish Minister for Sports, Amanda Lind, asked for town planning to ask themselves how often the child's perspective and their ability to interact with their surroundings was considered.

The three constraints approach recognises the socio-cultural constraints, such as organisational structures and the culture in and around youth sport. It becomes clear that the system remains the biggest obstacle.

The International Olympic Committee wrote a consensus in the *British Journal of Sports Medicine* in 2015 on youth athletic development. In it, they voiced their concerns about specialisation, the increased competitiveness of youth sport that led to increased physical development and inadequate time spent on rest and recovery as well as human development.

I believe that in football, the increased role of specialisation and the so-called 'race to the bottom', where teams are scouting players of ever younger ages in the hope of finding the next generational talent, has led the sport to a host of players who were rarely if ever holistically coached at a young age. The evidence shows that the two leading factors for children playing sport at a young age are fun and friendship. In most cases, early specialisation kills both of these factors because kids are often performing drills in an attempt to hone skills, and are in academies, away from their friends.

As professor, sports scientist and philosopher Dr. Richard Bailey argued on the *Learning in Development* podcast, the main issue is approaching this with the mindset that "children are mini adults."

"The reason for stating that children are not mini adults is that if we are coaching children we cannot simply adapt adult practises to small people. We have to start from the psychology and physiology of children and build coaching practises out of that. "

"Early specialisation seems to me the cruder version of ignoring the motto 'children are not mini adults' because that's a career we've launched them on. Early specialisation launches a sporting career. Even the word is an adult value."

For both those who leave the game early as a result of a system designed to expel the majority of them, and for the minority that do make it into the professional space, can we then in any way be surprised that many in both groups lack a stronger foundation as a result of negligible holistic coaching? Football has been so focussed on the development of players that it has too often neglected the person. Without holistic coaching, football has bred a generation of players ill-equipped to handle the pressures of life as both a professional athlete and a very public member of society.

Traditional linear development is problematic. Development of any kind in any field is built around a unique and ever-evolving foundation that includes physical growth, biological and behaviour development as well as their combined interactions. In short, people are individuals and must be considered that way.

At the end of the journal the IOC listed a number of recommendations for youth development, and they included the following suggestions for coaches:

- Establish meaningful relationships that enrich the personal assets of their athletes and foster their own interpersonal skills (e.g. reflection and communication).
- Seek interdisciplinary support and guidance in managing a young athlete's athletic development, fitness and health, and mental and social needs.

More generally, there was a call for the definition of success in sport to be broader, to centre development on both the athlete and the person, to commit to nurturing personal excellence, and throughout the development process help each athlete manage the sport-life balance better. For all of the IOC's shortcomings as an organisation, these recommendations about how to move forward in youth football deserve greater recognition than just being filed away in yet another academic paper on youth development. These are words to heed. If followed they can move us away from the often confined and linear approach that has long troubled youth sport.

That is not to say constraints are not necessary. For O'Sullivan, constraints are not negatives or positives, but neutral, understood as boundaries that can influence how an individual performs a task. These constraints change over time, at different time-scales. As they are critical factors in terms of development, they must always be considered. That is the choice the club has made and implementing such a philosophy is both brave and important. It places the child in the centre, it keeps multiple sport and other activities open rather than prematurely forcing children to specialise towards one ultimate goal that few will achieve (aka reaching the professional level). It also invites more representative learning opportunities in game forms and recognises the non-linearity of human development, which is a more accurate portrayal of life.

At the heart of this approach is a learner-based method. Rather than creating session plans focussed on one specific idea, the practice would generally be centred around situational exercises that have constraints that can be modified and manipulated. This enables the coach to create an environment where the players play the information in front of them instead of focussing on a rule or being limited to a pattern typical of many more traditional approaches.

There are also benefits from the coach's perspective to consider. Planning sessions has often become the topic of conversation in Swedish coaching circles.

AIK are challenging a culturally dominant planning paradigm that underpins many coach education programmes around the world. The coach decides the theme, breaks the session up into parts, decides how long each part will be and the order to deliver them in, and then the coach follows a list of pre-planned coaching points. "I have seen so many coaches, during coach education and out in their own practice, deliberately looking for these coaching points as opposed to focussing their attention on what is actually happening in front of them," O'Sullivan said.

At the moment, the premise of most session planning is built around focus and time. For example, a 20-minute session focussing on transitional play. However, if the focus of sessions were angled more towards observation and reflection then it might allow for more human development to occur in the most relatable place of all: the pitch. James Vaughan explained this to me perfectly, with the use of whiteboard, quite soon after I arrived at the academy.

The word 'drill' is problematic in sport. The most appropriate definition in this context is probably "a physical or mental exercise aimed at perfecting facility and skill especially by regular practice." However, as the brilliant Stuart Armstrong states throughout his work the drill approach is what kills creativity. So, Vaughan explained a modified game about overlaps in football.

On a narrow area in the centre of the field, Vaughan explained one key rule: whenever a player receives the ball facing forward between the lines of the field, zones out wide open up but only in front of the player with the ball. The result was that players naturally seek the overlap without having been told directly to do so. This is a fairly basic premise in coaching, to teach a skill without it being pointedly explained. However, the human benefit of this is creating people who are capable of solving problems or figuring out solutions themselves, a valuable skill whether your future lies in professional sport or not.

"So the task constraint (pitch area) changes in certain moments (facing forward between the lines) and shines a light on opportunities to use the high wide spaces," Vaughan tells me. "The idea being that players become attuned to these spaces in this moment and experiment with ways of exploiting the space. One example might be an overlap, but even working in this way is subject to socio-cultural and systemic constraints. When I and other AIK coaches designed this overlaps session on a UEFA course in Sweden, the course instructor asked after watching the session (in which there where many overlaps, through balls, channel runs) why we hadn't 'stated the topic' to the group at the start of the session. We looked at each other and one of my coaching colleagues simply said: 'Well that would have given them the answer and smart defenders will adapt and defend differently when they know that overlaps are the topic of the session.'

This is how we aim to work, and it can be quite different from what's taught by Sweden's national governing body. This makes it hard for us, as so many coaches look up to the Swedish football federation. This is a socio-cultural constraint that some of our more ambitious coaches face. They want to coach the socially accepted 'right' way, not the way that best meets the needs of the players."

One concern is that in their efforts to create opportunities for human development, the coaches rarely get time to consider their own work. It was perhaps telling that some of the coaches at AIK told me that it was only when they spoke to or received feedback from people outside of the project that they were made aware of what they were really doing and how different it was from the norm.

"I do not want AIK to be jewellery for people," Hörtin says of parents who might see the famous club as an opportunity to leverage either their own or their child's social status. The club is there to help kids make decisions about their own development. In one of the meetings with the children while talking to them about their options, Hörtin put the kids at the front and the parents at the back so as to make it clear he was talking to the children.

In a co-authored 2018 letter in response to an article published in the *Journal of Sports Science & Medicine* that was investigating biological maturity and the relative age effect in young footballers, O'Sullivan and Andrew Kirkland explained why they believed there was no such thing as an elite international under-nine soccer player. Their letter was met with a response from the author of the original paper which included the following: *"we called the participants of the U9 Eurochampionship 2016 in Vienna 'elite international U9 soccer players' and we don't understand what is wrong with this."*

Clearly, if it is not a problem for academics in the profession of sport science and youth development to use the word 'elite' in connection with nine-year-olds then it is no surprise that this language becomes more common. Even at such young ages, it allows for some parents to be seduced by the concept of something that sounds close to the professional world of sport often seen on the television (even though the truth is worlds away).

AIK's hope is to reduce player transitions, as they believe children feel their best staying in their home environment for as long as possible. Player transitions are too often a result of parents keen on the social status that comes with having a "successful child". It is worth taking time to think about that last sentence and the real weight it carries. Many parents are not this way inclined, but the subconscious culture of silent judgement of social status is an alarming issue.

The same level of concern rises from the presence of the virtual world. The desire to have a profile that displays which league you're playing in suddenly puts social status and the image of being one step closer to the professional game in the foreground. If 13-year-olds are not only aware of the concept of image but are also developing it in a virtual space that often gets blurred with the real world, a web of complexity arrives. A shot of dopamine later, and the addiction begins.

A study published in *Psychological Science, The Power of the Like in Adolescence*, a journal of the Association for Psychological Science, revealed that when teenagers see large numbers of likes on their own photos or the photos of peers on a social network, it stimulates the same brain circuits activated when eating chocolate and winning money.

Likes are a virtual representation of social acceptance, of approval in the social space. And if they can become a source of financial income, suddenly the world of social media goes from something young people do for leisure to a weapon of mass destruction. Internal development, emotional understanding, and organic growth is sacrificed for a virtual space that feeds off your well-being.

Creating a virtual image is now more of an issue because young players consider it a further - perhaps even necessary - step towards professionalism. This is a major concern. A desire to professionalise and commodify everything in society today, as part of the mega-capitalist push for endless growth, has spread into youth football. AIK are fighting to change that, putting the focus back on the well-being of the children, but they too are battling against long-standing structures.

David Snowden is a smart man. The Welshman works in management consultancy and is considered one of the leading thinkers in the field of complexity. Snowden is perhaps best known for the Cynefin framework, a structure he created whilst working for IBM that effectively makes you consider the impact of your situation when making a decision, so as to avoid simply approaching something the same way as always. There are five contexts: Obvious, Complicated, Chaotic, Complex and Disorder. The complex context is the most interesting because it is the most applicable to human development. What Snowden's framework suggests is that rather than trying to control a situation or insist on an approach it is best to look for patterns and encourage the emergence of a solution.

Part of the issue is the desire, and not just in football, to find an approach and stick to it. There so often needs to be a numerical value to what we do in football, proof on paper that we can use as evidence of our work. Speaking at a TEDx Talk in 2018, Snowden said the following: *"If you look at the whole history of the last 40 to 50 years, everything has to have a target, everything has to have a defined outcome - and it has to be a number."*

This pursuit of tangible results is widespread in football, and is one of the largest hurdles human development faces. Human development is harder to see, which means it is easy to discard. Speed, strength, reactions - these are all areas of ability that are now easy to measure. The steps human beings take though, are much harder to map because numbers cannot be applied. Ironically, years after their creation, the Myers–Briggs models and the colours to reflect personality type have perhaps done more damage in creating boxes to put people in. The beauty of humans is that they are unpredictable and not easy to understand. They are complex systems, and in the world of football what you end up having is a host of individual complex systems trying to survive inside one larger complex system.

It is Snowden who knows best about complex systems. In the same TEDx Talk, Snowden discusses the different types of system and the importance of one, the complex adaptive system. This approach is defined by connectivity, placing value on relationship and day-to-day interactions. This is perfectly in line with what AIK are trying to do, and given the inherently complex nature of any kind of development it is baffling that so many are constantly looking for either a numerical answer or a simplified approach to a system that is too complex to crunch.

Developmental psychologist Urie Bronfenbrenner created a theory called the ecology of human development, the idea being that a person's development is shaped over time by the interactions between the individual and their environment. The concept that individuals develop within a system of relationships to family, school, community and society, and not in isolation, is totally logical and speaks to much of the work being done by AIK in Sweden.

While in Stockholm, I was also able to meet PhD research

scholar and coach Scott Swainston. Scott was investigating the transition of academy players into the first team and explained to me a system he had tested with a club in England. He arranged for six players - three who got first team contracts and three who didn't - to record weekly video diaries for 40 weeks. Afterwards, he also conducted four interviews to check in with the players and how they felt. The recordings revealed their change in understanding and perception as they developed or as their situation changed, but most interestingly it ended up providing an opportunity for the players to talk, effectively to themselves, through their emotions. Just the chance to do that made a huge difference to their understanding of the situation and gave them the privacy and safety to be able to discuss their feelings in a way that might not have been possible otherwise.

My initial understanding of human development had been restricted. Now, sitting on the train back to Copenhagen with the sunset spilling out across the green landscape, I was engaging with another level of understanding. Human development was also something that could be coaxed out through a values-based environment. If everyday behaviours match the values of the organisation then there is a far greater chance of those values being alive. Snowden said that there is "no valid model of a human system but the system itself." It is time to embrace the complexity.

3

Germany

In full kit, coming out of the changing rooms and playing on a pitch on the club's grounds, it is hard to look at an U12s team as just a group of 11-year-olds playing football. Of course, playing for professional teams demands a higher standard but whoever the club, there's no denying this environment entices you to forget that those who are playing are children.

The play occasionally looks like football but still retains a lot of the childish nature of the early stages of playing a sport. Some kids sometimes run so fast they fall over, other times the play is scrappy as the ball is won and lost in quick succession. And then, either as a result of a sweeping team move or a moment of individual brilliance, someone stands out. This is why many coaches agree that talent identification at anything below 14 is flawed. If you saw one 12-year-old at the right moment that might be enough to convince you they were a talent. If you saw the same one in the wrong ten minutes you might think they had no chance of becoming a professional. That is not only a flawed system, but an unfair one that undoubtedly lets a great deal of potential slip away.

As was evident from the academy work I saw in Sweden, the decision to change academy structures to allow for later development has many benefits. It not only impacts a child's chances of becoming a professional athlete, but also affects their growth as a person. Sadly, power-hungry individuals and limiting structures can turn the focus of an academy towards results and numbers, confining those coaches with the right intentions and leaving the children, who are rarely the problem, to suffer.

"It shouldn't really matter in the youth arena but it does; what was an education environment has become a business environment and I don't think we will ever get away from that now," a Bundesliga academy coach told me on the phone in the summer of 2020, requesting anonymity.

"I can't speak for others but I constantly have to check myself because it's very easy to slide into the common behaviours of some of those around you, the environment, the culture of football generally... I have to keep asking myself all the time, 'Is that the right thing to do?'. I've had to compromise a little bit because in order for the kids to survive and for the coach to survive you have to make some decisions that feel questionable but necessary. This then gives you some freedom to undertake some of the activities that are important for the holistic development of the player, but less focussed on short term results. Deep down I know it is not right, but you feel compelled to do it nevertheless. It is a real fight with the conscience at times."

One example the coach tells me is from when he first started and was asked to coach in another language so as to help teach the kids to improve their language skills during their time at football. Results though, got in the way.

"Over half of the boys were new to academy football, the coaching team was new, and it was a new format progressing from the small-sided game. However, after three months and with the team not winning all the time, it was decided to resort to only German coaching again with the thought that it would improve the team's fortunes. The coordinator didn't actually state it was 'because you're not winning every week' but it was in the air."

At the time, the coach sent out a questionnaire to parents and players about how they felt about sessions in another language to supplement what they learnt at school. The results were overwhelmingly positive but he nevertheless had to do the sessions solely in German for a few months. Ironically, years later, he would have no problem returning to his original approach. "Now I'm doing exactly the same and I speak in English a lot of the time but because the team is more successful it draws little attention. It had nothing to do with the language but it is a small example of how decisions can be based on results even at youth level. What is a shame is that it was never celebrated how greatly their language skills improved; by the end I did not need to speak German and they would understand everything. For some of them, this skill and subconsciously learning football vocabulary in an international language may prove invaluable."

Appearances can be deceiving, sadly. For every club that says all the right things, very few practise what they preach.

"You won't get anybody from any club who will dispute what we should be doing and that scores are largely irrelevant for long term development. I think some behave in the belief they're doing the right thing, but if you had personal conversations with coaches then perhaps they'd admit that team results do affect their behaviour more than it should at times."

With the demands on their time it's no surprise that coaches want to focus on the thing they'll be judged mostly on, namely the football. But for most of the kids, football won't be what they end up doing so why is the focus not on developing them as people so as to equip them with transferable life skills?

Coaches, particularly at the academy level, shouldn't have to win a few games in order to gain themselves enough leeway with their bosses to incorporate more character development into training. For some though, that is the reality. It's about results because results are tangible and equate to a logical but narrow definition of success. The U12s won 12 games this year so that means a lot of things must be going right. It's a simple equation, but by only using some of the information the wrong conclusions are drawn.

Winning needs to take a back seat, not football. By focussing on personal development, especially at younger ages, fun is retained and the skills that will help children in life, both professionally and privately, are developed. Each coach will take a different approach in how to develop these skills, considering the players, parents, the environment and the time they have together. The foundation the academy coach I spoke to certainly seemed a good place for many to start.

"It's about taking a broader view of the individual's development. There is so much structure within formalised coaching from such a young age, that it is easy to lose sight of the value of the informal and spontaneous non-football interactions that can make a big difference," he said. "At the centre of it is making the kids feel like they're steering the process. If the players decide the positive behaviours they would like to see, they are more likely to buy into the process. With the behaviours established, we then draw a line under those behaviours and visually show that those chosen behaviours equal success. Behaviours that fall then below the line, when regularly shown, mean that your chances of achieving your aims (success) become less, not greater. It is very simple but for the kids it's very tangible. All that is left for the coach to do is to provide opportunities in a footballing and non-footballing context to allow them to practise the good behaviours."

The key with children is to remember that what follows the learning aim is most important. They understand what they want to work towards but the real key is helping them understand what they need to do on a daily basis in order to achieve those aims.

That is why the value of activities or trips where kids are given the opportunity to learn and develop organisational skills or teamwork is priceless. Buying food for the group, making their own beds even when staying in hotels, cleaning the changing rooms or even washing up might seem like trivial or minor exercises. But in a group setting for an away game or tournament trip, they are the small changes that can make a major difference. Any yet for many professional football clubs, the implementation of character development activities is a decision not considered important.

"Coaches have certain freedom to dictate their programmes, but I believe it is more and more difficult because clubs are wary of being seen to be doing something wrong. They get more conservative because they feel they have to. They are particularly nervous about the influence of social media. If something negative is posted on social media it's a real nightmare for the whole club, so it is no surprise many would rather not take the risk of doing something that is standard and safe. Unfortunately, the consequence of this is that the kids miss out because everything becomes very structured, very ordinary and dare I say it a bit dull."

Dullness does not sharpen anything. It is hard to imagine any organisation, a football club or a business or a school, that will succeed at developing people with a structure that suffocates rather than guides.

"The danger for all large organisations, not just football clubs, is bureaucracy and complacency, and this is compounded when traditions make it very difficult to question what has always been. It's a danger because what the modern working environment needs and demands is that people are very flexible, adaptable and creative to find solutions under extreme pressure. If we consider the most successful people of our generation, one would notice that they have these qualities in abundance. Modern companies value innovation and the culture of challenging the status quo to react immediately to fast-changing environments. This is particularly difficult for clubs steeped in traditions. I guess newer clubs like Hoffenheim and RB Leipzig find this culture much easier to embrace."

Even the structure of development is often confined. While there are challenges in incorporating such a practice with young age groups, the older the children get the smaller the chances are.

"It's very difficult in the older age groups because the players are already starting to earn money and have contracts with sporting brands. They start to feel like a professional, the consequence being that we create a rod for our own backs.," the coach tells me.

In England, clubs work with organisations such as the LFE (League Football Education) to "deal with this rod."

The LFE, perhaps aided by operating in a somewhat different world to the Premier League, is admittedly doing some fantastic work, largely in academies. Clubs are connecting with communities to create workshops and activities that further personal development, while others hand over complete control to the players for games, allowing them to organise travel, tactics and team-talks. This promotes responsibility and ownership, skills that extend well beyond the pitch.

Originally established in 2004 to help teenagers in the Football League with apprenticeship programmes such as coaching badges or educational skills, the LFE has since expanded its coverage to players between U9 and U23, parents and club staff, as well as broadening its services to include aspects such as emotional well-being, resilience and personal development. Simon Williams, in charge of the LFE's life skills, has done some great work using the framework of why, how and what to help make the approach relatable to young people rather than just another classroom format. Williams and the LFE team are making bold and necessary steps to look after the individual by being engaged with people and not just players.

"The problem is, however good the course is, the kids still see it as a course," the aforementioned academy coach tells me. "So they go to a workshop for two hours and they tick that off in their folder but it's not necessarily followed upon a day-to-day basis. It's patchwork, but then it is not easy for a coach or a club. The modern young player has so many influences including sponsors, agents, family members (who may not always have the child's best interest at heart), teachers, friends. The players need more mentors than coaches at times."

The confined structure of doing activities for the sake of them hampers the true reason for adopting human development, and without a follow-up the activities become isolated inside an age group rather than part of a progressive development that matches your time at the club. This leads to the current monster model, where first-teams are quick to appoint player care officers but not character development coaches. The appropriate implementation of a player care department helps the player both in life and growth, in turn helping the club too. However, if not done correctly and with the wrong people, player care can also end up being a facilitator of ease that might not help as much as first thought. Teams are naturally desperate to make sure their professionals have everything they need sorted for them so that they can just focus on the football, but in doing so they also infantilise their players.

Indeed, too much of professional sport has gone so far beyond an understanding of what makes a healthy person that when college quarterback star Trevor Lawrence told *Sports Illustrated* that "it's not like I need this for my life to be okay" he was met with questions about his desire to excel. Honestly, what a remarkable turn of events in which a mature young man reveals that while he loves football, success in that field is not going to make or break him and yet in doing so is met with questions about whether he wants it enough. Lawrence ended up taking to Twitter to further explain himself, outlining that he is "secure in who I am and what I believe. I don't need football to make feel worthy as a person. I purely love the game."

This is an attitude we should be cheering for and not questioning. Every person is different and comes from a different context. To question a man who is mature enough to admit he loves the game but that it won't define him deserves respect. What is most ironic is that Lawrence is considered one of the most talented college players in his position. It is no coincidence that he is also perhaps one of the most mature.

"Clubs do appoint people to cater to the needs of the player but again there is a balance to be reached. If you take away too much responsibility from the players in order to avoid pitfalls and problems, then essentially all you do is cover up potential cracks in the player's character development. Most parents will admit that there is sometimes a fine line between support that stifles and support that enables. There is of course also the issue of no support, but that does not always result in a negative outcome. If the players aren't learning how to handle situations or to think for themselves or to manage things, then they will not be ideally prepared for what awaits them in the real world. Essentially we are talking about the development of values, such as resilience responsibility and many more. If we get the balance wrong we need to ask ourselves what kind of person are we creating long term."

The absence of character development at an older age group because the business starts to take centre stage can sever the tie between growing and developing. Granted, it becomes harder because the expectation is so strongly tied to performance but is it not unfair to expect players to perform if they're only being developed in a sporting sense?

Often young teenagers break into the first team, play well and see their value sky rocket. Is this not an incredible time of change in a young person's life? If all they have is a couple of years of character development from when they were 12 to rely on, or worse none at all, then how is this a healthy approach? Put in the language of the modern boardroom, is this even effective and sensible asset management?

Furthermore, why is character development on offer to young people hoping to become professional players if the moment that is achieved the development no longer continues? It just doesn't make any sense.

"The way the game is going at the moment, kids are going into the professional arena younger and younger. They're joining an adult and professional environment when they're still kids really and then you're reliant on the network around that person... Not every player has a strong family support."

If character development is built into a club's philosophy, where relationships take a hold and the concept of development is continual, flexible and adaptable then it is possible for effects to be long-standing. Furthermore, players who then make the first team are less likely to feel ill-equipped for the changes in their life. They will have a guide - not a butler - to help them through these situations.

The reason this approach is often ignored is not simply because it lacks the kind of results that look good in a boardroom, but also because it is not an easy thing to do. There are no shortcuts to this approach. It takes time and care to look after each individual in a specific way.

"It's difficult. It's not very tangible. Takes a lot of effort and time and a lot of energy, particularly as it has to be on an individual basis. In order to see the results of the work you need a lot of time, and coaches only get their team for a year or two and so are more interested on the football side of things because that's where they're judged."

The coronavirus pandemic certainly changed the game for football coaches across the world, and in some ways forced judgement of their coaching to change too.

The coach encouraged the players to develop their own training schedule each week based upon learning targets they had chosen for themselves. The plan included a games console league, a fun art competition, stay-at-home challenges and Skype sessions where players would check in with one another and their coach. While their efforts being recorded and converted into points sadly exemplifies the perhaps inevitable sliding into some form of competition, it is commendable to see such effort from coaches during such an unprecedented and difficult time.

Indeed, that was just the tip of the iceberg. The coach of this team showed me the plan he had created to help his team out during the pandemic. The aim was to help the boys make the most of the situation and to provide them with a sense of security and hope. He understood what Generation Z children needed and how they best responded. The coach's approach was built from recognising they had gained time, and how that was not just a chance for technical development but also character growth. Through support, fun activities, regular contact, some competition and the chance to take further ownership of their own development, the observations were telling. The coach reported a spike in creativity, motivation and responsibility. Although difficult to evaluate, he also believed that through more interaction it helped the majority of boys to cope with the situation. Of course, the approach had its challenges too as not being able to provide live feedback was difficult, as was managing the dynamics of team play, technological difficulties and helping kids with homework when there was sometimes a lack of support and feedback from schools. Nevertheless, it was an example of how even during the most testing times for the planet, there are ways to be innovative in coaching and many of them are directly connected to the development of the person rather than the technical ability of the player.

When working with children the determining factor is remembering they are children and not professionals in the making. Finland international Tim Sparv once wrote something similar on his website: "We need to stop being so eager to win when we're dealing with kids. Our priorities need to change so that we can give our youth the best possible environment to be in. An environment where kids can be kids."

The 34-year-old Finn is a seasoned pro. After making the jump from his homeland to play in Southampton's youth team, Sparv went on to play in first teams in Germany, Sweden, the Netherlands, Denmark and Greece. A month before his contract ended with AEL in Greece and two months before he captained Finland at their first ever European Championships we had a conversation. By the end of it there was no doubt an intriguing and remarkable book about his time in Greece would be on the way, but it was Sparv's experiences in football that left a deeper mark. His time in the game was a reminder of how much more there is to each person's story than appears on the surface or the CV, and how quickly the game has changed when it comes to human development.

"I feel that we're talking more about this kind of approach today than we did maybe 15 years ago, when I first started," Sparv explains. "It was a lot about your performance on the pitch, your physical attributes. We did not maybe talk about what was happening between your ears as much as we do today. I feel like there's definitely some clubs doing it really well. They have that holistic approach and they think about the whole human being, not only about games and training. When we are so young, when we first come up and the extreme pressures and expectations that we're surrounded by, they will have a negative influence on you not only as a footballer but also as a human. I felt it was tough, especially when I was trying to make the step up from academy football to professional football. All of a sudden it was somehow so much more serious. It wasn't about development in the same way anymore. It was about getting points. It was about being pragmatic. It was about playing defensive football, winning duels. I didn't really understand that part and I had a really tough time dealing with these setbacks that every one of us had to deal with at some point, like in January, sitting on the bench, not feeling like the coach understands you. But that wasn't someone else's fault. It was me. I didn't really have the skills to navigate those kind of issues. I didn't know really what to do. I always felt I was strong enough to deal with it myself, but I wasn't. It took me too long to actually understand that this is part of sports and part of football, and I needed to deal with it in a more mature way. I needed to get those tools, whatever they might be. I was not a good listener back then. I always felt like my opinion was the best and I knew best and I wouldn't really take other people's assessment of me. I had people around me trying to help but when you're closed off to yourself, you're just not open to other people's feedback so that was a very frustrating time."

The late teenage years are so critical for both player and personal development, and as Sparv explains it's about much more than being able to pass and move as well as the first team. It's about understanding how to navigate as an adult in a first-team changing room, especially when playing in a foreign country.

"It's so difficult because there's a change of dressing room and you know the jokes are a little bit sturdier and that can take its toll on you somehow. And if you don't know how to navigate in that world, it will be really difficult. But the younger generation, they're more open about their own mental health issues, they show weakness in a way that was a little bit taboo for myself. I didn't want to tell anyone else that I was struggling. I couldn't, because that would somehow maybe influence other people's judgment of me and then I worried whether I was going to get game time after that," Sparv says, adding that much has changed since he played. Nutrition, sleep and mental health were topics that either randomly came up in meetings (and were not followed up) or never came up at all. Things are different now.

"There is a different generation coming through and maybe also because of the environment that we are creating, there's more focus on mental health... I'm not saying that they [clubs who develop holistically] do it perfectly, but they are definitely trying to take care of the whole human being. I think you always have to have that in mind, especially as a coach or anyone working with young kids. You're not just preparing them for life as a footballer, but you're actually preparing them for a life in society."

The well-documented and aforementioned short-term thinking in football does not lend itself to holistic development. As Sparv said, results are the name of the game, and that environment breeds impatience and a craving for success. Such is the powerful nature of sports like football that total avoidance of this environment throughout a career is near impossible, but there are places and people who have realigned their focus so that success is a byproduct rather than the aim. In Sweden, AIK is a club that does this well. In Denmark, the same can be said for Nordsjælland. During his six years at Midtjylland, Sparv found another Danish club aware of the need to develop the person.

"We would go into the forests," Sparv said of the team-building activities that he participated in. "We would leave our phones and everything. We had just a very basic package and would sleep in tents and there would be crappy weather and it would really, really bring us closer together. We would do all these kind of different assignments and we would make a barbecue, stay by the fireplace and talk about life. It's really tough because you wouldn't sleep for a couple of days and it was a real psychological challenge. But when you got through it, when you came out the other side, it felt so good and you would have something to talk about for the coming years."

Sparv also recalled another trip involving terrible weather, skis and climbing up a mountain. Amusingly enough, the forest trip he described came in his first year at the club, which just so happened to be the first time Midtjylland won the Danish league title in the club's history. There were endless factors that contributed to that victory but clearly bringing that group of people closer together certainly did their performance as players no harm.

"It's not only about going out for meals and then going bowling or something, but it could be these kind of trips where you come close to nature and you force people to put down their phones and just actually be together for 24 hours," Sparv says, admitting that as a nature-lover this comes easier to him, while still seeing value in such trips regardless of preference. Perhaps it was easier for Sparv because of where he came from. Long before he was camping in Danish forests the Finn had experienced the foundation for balancing life and sport. There was no ruthlessness to seeking a career in professional football in Finland at that time and it turns out playing football in rural Finland is as idyllic as it sounds.

"The environment that I was in was very, very low key," Sparv says of playing football in his youth. "We were just friends playing together. I had my dad as a coach and I come from a very small village on the west coast. Maybe two thousand people live in my village but it was a very sports crazy environment, because in the summer we did athletics, football, and then it was anything in the winter. That's part of our life. But it was never an insane eagerness to become a professional athlete. It was more like fun and play."

Sparv realised early on what it took if he wanted to become a professional footballer and so worked hard to train. He might have changed but the environment stayed the same.

"I was always training on my own, at home, running in forests, you know, staying home during the weekends and training. I was always about that goal ahead of me and I knew what I had to do to make it, but still the whole environment was more like a family thing. You know, we would go to these tournaments in Finland and Sweden and we would take our families with us. We'd take a big bus or two and we would go to different places and it would be like this very family-friendly trip together," Sparv said before adding with a smile that it was also fun because he and his team would normally win as well. The group feeling though, was what mattered more. "We would stay at a camping place in these small, small wooden houses and it would be like just a very, very cool, cool experience. For us as children, we wanted to win but the atmosphere made it special."

Manchester United's academy director Nick Cox talked about the importance of the right environment and how he and his team cultivate that. Cox's approach and beliefs are undoubtedly in a great place when it comes to holistic development, but working at one of the biggest football clubs in the world also means battling on a number of fronts.

Around March 2021, the club advertised a position for a Lead Phase Scout for 6-8 year-olds. On his website *The Talent Equation* Stuart Armstrong delivered a scathing review of how the commodification of language has led professional clubs "to use the language of the market when talking about human children."

Indeed, Armstrong's beliefs are echoed by clubs like AIK and many coaches and players out there who believe that the so-called "race to the bottom" (clubs scouting and acquiring players from younger and younger ages in the hope of them becoming first-team players or sources of profit) is a maddening and unhealthy development in youth football. They believe children should be left to be children for as long as possible. As a child who ran in Finnish forests and as a player who believes clubs should never forget their community and the people working for it, Tim Sparv unsurprisingly feels the same.

"I feel strongly about this thing that is happening now that we're scouting nine, ten, 11-year-olds, trying to create this hyper-professional environment where it's all about competition and the enjoyment and fun is taken out of it. The career path that we're selecting kids on at the age of 11 and 12 and thinking we've seen something, something that will make them into a professional football... I just feel up until 14, 15, 16, it doesn't need to be [that way]. Of course you need to work but that whole atmosphere should be about trying to create that long term involvement in sport. If you get a good start I think you'll stay in football in some way, and there's so many guys from my own childhood in that team I was playing for still playing today at different levels. I play here and in the national team, but I still have friends that play sixth, fifth or fourth division in Finland and they just love it."

Unlike most of his friends from childhood, Sparv has undoubtedly made a career out of football but that those friendships have remained 20 years later speaks to Sparv's character. When he played in Germany or the Netherlands sometimes his friends would come over to visit. When he returns to Finland every year, whether during summer or at Christmas, the group gets together. Sometimes when he's home he goes and watches their games. "Fifth, sixth division in Finland, that's where the real football is," he says with a grin.

Sparv will always cherish his 83 caps for his country and the Europa League appearances, but what matters most are those friendships. While it's only natural for some of our childhood friends to drift away with time, in professional sports as ruthless as football the environment often creates competition at all times, making your teammates someone you have to beat. Too much of the system isn't designed for those relationships to be maintained and while rural Finland might be an easier place to start than others, it is Sparv's ability to maintain those friendships that says a lot more about him than his trophies or international appearances. And at the end of it all, that's exactly how it should be and probably how he'd like it.

4

England

Nick Cox isn't a fan of human development suddenly becoming the new buzzword in coaching.

"Coaching and human development are one and the same thing. Coaching is personal connections, relationships, trust. Human development is not a nice addition, it is part of it. The skill of coaching is about personal connection," the Manchester United academy director says to me on a Zoom call during the second coronavirus lockdown.

Cox is the ultimate embodiment of human development. Such is his attentive nature that to find time when he wasn't answering calls from parents, listening to the concerns of one of the academy boys or discussing plans with a coach was difficult. Even then, the buzz and ping of his phone still echoed in the background of our chat.

It's understandable. Despite meeting in a virtual setting, Cox is friendly, engaging and personable. Truly charismatic people can reach through the virtual world and resonate beyond the sound in your ears and the sight on your screen.

In a football world that is increasingly struggling to feel genuine, it is hard not to feel refreshed after talking to Cox. Manchester United has a famous history with developing players. During the lockdown Marcus Rashford proved the club has done a great job developing people too, the striker taking on the UK government in the summer of 2020 to put meals in the bellies of hungry children. Speaking to Cox, it becomes apparent how and why the focus on the human is so prevalent at the club. It starts by reaching beyond the widespread understanding of what an academy is for.

"It's always understood the academy's measure of success to a certain degree is individual development, which can be measured in debuts," Cox says. "That's still a bit clinical, though. I think you have to a higher existence than debuts, just like the best football teams in the world have to have a higher existence than winning. It's about how we win and what values do we win by. An academy has to have a higher existence than developing and generating debuts. And that higher existence for me is about creating an amazing addition to childhood, creating memories and experiences that will enrich lives, regardless of what the outcome is so if you don't become a footballer you still reflect on the experience as one that enriched you and you were better for. And the time you dedicated means you still have some tangible stuff that you can take with you on your journey wherever you end up, knowing it was an amazing launchpad for adult life."

Simply hearing the words 'higher existence' in a conversation about football was refreshing. Naturally, such conversations are easier to have in academies, which by their nature are not under the same pressure or scrutiny as first teams. However, it has been well-documented that in recent years pressure on academies has reached dangerous levels as professionalism has extended its claws further and further down the age groups. Once the idea of the game has been delivered it cannot be undelivered, unsaid or unsold. Once the tracksuit is on the 11-year-old, it is impossible not only to get it off but to remove the ideas that settle with it.

Manchester United's youth teams obviously want to win and they're going to be competitive, but there is a methodology to their pursuit of winning rather than just blindly pursuing the incentive that sport has long dined out on. The sheer achievement of winning alone is not what sport is or has ever been about, and that Manchester United have not only recognised that but implemented an approach around that recognition is particularly exciting.

Cox believes the key is to make sure the importance of winning is that you yourself dictate the factors for victory.

"It's up to us to decide when we arrange a fixture which of development, performance and competition are going to be the most important focus for the day. Sometimes we will decide the objective today is the result because that's going to be a test of everything we've learned and whether we can perform in a competitive environment, i.e. do we know how to manage a game? That may be determined by the age of the player, the competition which we're in, the stage of the season, the group of players we are. We're always going to be competitive, we're always going to play to win, but we are going to do it in such a way we won't compromise the way in which we do it, so some games are about development - express yourself, try new things."

Admittedly, given the means at their disposal this approach is easier for a club of Manchester United's stature to take. But with those means and the club's prestige also comes a certain degree of expectation. The club's remarkable run of games with academy players involved is proof they are meeting that expectation. That they are doing so with an approach that clearly incorporates the development of young people is monumental.

To achieve this, Cox has to do a lot of juggling. "You've got to use a fixture as a tool in your development and decide what the onus is going to be. The difficult bit is managing the expectation of the people around you."

Cox has to convince the board of this approach, players who might be confused by an approach that on the one hand says be competitive but on the other says the result isn't important, and parents who want their child to be the best player in a winning team.

"It's my duty to make sure every now and again that a player is that, but that's a very one-dimensional diet," Cox says of kids being the best player in a winning team. "We get some kids who don't get to be the best player in a winning team and if that's the case I've got it wrong, and we've got some players who are the best player in a winning team every week and we've got it wrong there as well. You've got to manipulate the experiences, the fixtures you're involved in, the team you play for and the people you play with so that whether you're the best or weakest player, you're in a winning or losing team, you're in a game where you can express yourself or one where you're going to struggle, you've seen it all. If that happens, when you get to Old Trafford under pressure, whatever happens you can say, 'I've seen something that looks like this before and it's cool and I can deal with this.'"

Cox believes that as a result of the formative nature of our football experiences everyone from fans to players is wired up to believe in the binary approach that winning is good, losing is bad. In Cox's academy at Manchester United, it is not that binary.

"It's not 'winning good losing bad' because you know what, losing can be really good sometimes and winning sometimes can be bad. I've got to rewire everyone so that you can understand what you've been brought up with is different to what we're doing. Most of the kids you will have recruited will have come out of a grassroots team where they won every week and got trophies and medals. That's got you here and now I have to rewire you and rewiring people is really, really difficult, particularly coming up against organisations that have a different approach to winning."

Cox nearly stops himself but it becomes clear that something is gnawing at him. Clearly there is a team he has in mind that has a different approach to winning and although he doesn't explicitly say it the story he then retells makes it clear who he means.

Four years ago, in an U14s match Manchester United lost 9-0 to Manchester City. The result made the news on Sky Sports. The result is tough to take, but it was more the ripples it and the media coverage sent that were harder to contend with.

"We have to deal with that because that makes the board nervous, it makes parents nervous," Cox says. "How do I deal with this? Well guess what, Mason Greenwood played for us that night so who really won? The coach that night is now the coach of our U23 team so who really won in terms of development?"

There is certainly some bite to Cox's voice, and understandably. He is someone in an important position of power in world football where his choices can result in impactful change. That his assessment of such a loss is to see the long-term result for the club speaks volumes. Cox's message here is that both the professional and personal development of people inside the club matters much more than results.

So how does Cox actually implement this at Manchester United? I had learned about a values-based environment, I had seen how human development could be done through a curriculum, but how does one of the biggest clubs in the world do it?

Naturally, Manchester United combine the classic workshop, experience approach with the everyday behaviours that sound familiar to AIK.

The former is simply designed to give the kids a skill that will help them later in life, such as cooking or learning a language. The project aspect of this approach is intriguing though because, if done correctly, it opens the door for clubs to use what is unique to them as a learning tool. Naturally, Cox has recognised this.

"Every year we think it's important our boys understand Munich so our U13s met Jimmy Murphy Jr and they went around the museum," Cox says. "They spent time understanding what Munich meant for the football club, perhaps not so much Munich but the ten years after it and how that affects the experience you're now having and whose footsteps you are following in. The boys wrote poems and read them aloud at a Munich memorial ceremony and that isn't so much about knowing about Munich but rather standing up and reading a poem in front of 3,000 people, which is not a bad skill to have."

Therein lies perhaps the perfect example of how to combine a club's legacy and values into learning lessons that will impact long beyond a playing career. Jimmy Murphy Jr's father was not only the man who steadied the club during its greatest crisis but was also in charge of the club's youngsters. His history is important because it laid the groundwork for the legacy and fame the club retains in the modern era. That Manchester United's youngest learn about this is tremendously powerful for their understanding of what it means to play for the club and the city, but as Cox pointed out, it also gave them an opportunity to investigate concepts of identity and mortality as well as develop skills such as public speaking.

Cox also told me about a project that got the boys creating their own Walter Tull museum in honour of the man who had to give up his football career to fight in World War One, where he became recognised as the first black officer to lead white British solders into battle.

"The boys actually created their own museum and became the curators of it," Cox says. "We then had a magical moment where the first team had finished training and the players and staff came to our museum and our U12s curated. It was a powerful experience on every level."

Nothing is as powerful as the impact everyday behaviours can have. Cox recognises Manchester United's privileged position as a club means that funding is not an issue and tour locations are theirs to choose from, but the determination to retain learning in the face of privilege is pivotal to the development of people.

"The rest of it is how are we going to be every time we walk into the building, in terms of how we conduct ourselves, the respect we show each other, the way my coach communicates with me, how we empower our kids, asking them to present," Cox says of the more subtle aspects of the approach.

"For some kids it may just be the experience of being associated to a professional organisation where you are having to show commitment to a cause, understand routine and be professional wearing the correct uniform, arriving somewhere on time, understanding the rules and politics of an organisation," Cox says, before admitting that the younger you go with this association there is a case to be made that something healthy becomes unhealthy.

But there is no escaping the fact that an association with and a commitment to an organisation can change children's lives.

"Some kids might come from a world where they might never

have eaten dinner round a table so we might just be that. For some it may be that they don't have a male role model in their life, with us they have a coach. It probably means different things to different people. It might just be the one place in their week where they are deemed to be successful on a regular basis, or it's the place where they feel safe or where they're regularly engaging with the thing they love doing. That alone can be important for personal development."

Development is not just down to one person, or even a group of people, but rather the atmosphere they create. Cox is quick to acknowledge the impact of long-standing academy coaches Tony Whelan and Dave Bushell for being the "cultural architects" of the current academy. The key to their approach was to make it all about the kids rather than the kids' potential.

"I sometimes think the value of a young person in an academy - not at our place but I have witnessed it - is proportional to their ability" Cox says. "Tony and Dave are completely blind to kids' ability. If you're in the building and you're registered with us, you're getting unequivocal love regardless of ability, and that is a skill and not one that is very commonplace. They are as passionate about the kids that have left us as they are about the ones who go on to make debuts."

The long-standing impact of this for the coaches is that they will always be there, even long after those children have left childhood behind. The reason that even after all those years Cox and coaches with the same passion and empathy as him do answer the phone is that greatest of emotions, the driving force for so much change, the one emotion we cannot live without: love.

"As I said earlier, coaching is about connection, rapport, love, trust, high challenge, high support, which gives me the right to challenge, push and put you into environments that might be uncomfortable," Cox says. "The love and connection you build means that if someone picks the phone up ten years later, you have no choice but to say 'of course I can help.' I think how people behave after they've left your organisation is a marker of success. The real marker though is how the ones who didn't succeed as footballers interpret their experience with you. If your measure of success is debuts then you're in trouble. Debuts need to be the byproduct of success. What is success? Success is a positive healthy journey whether they arrive for a six-week trial or they are with you for ten years."

Most coaches almost certainly believe in personal development, but as Cox astutely says, "their behaviours might tell you something different." As mentioned earlier, structures and cultural expectations of organisations can cut a coach's passion for personal development. Often in high-performance sport, a results-focussed environment leaves no space for personal development. Language such as winning, producing, delivering replaces the likes of development, pleasure, personal. There is seemingly no escape.

But when we look back at our lives it is often not what but who that we remember, or at least the what we did lives stronger in the memory when it is tied to the people we shared the experience with.

"All these years later, I cannot remember a session I delivered or a scoreline, but I do remember every child and a bit about them," Cox says, with words that ring true for almost every profession.

Indeed, football has become much more than just coaching young people how to play a game. It has become an education, a way of life, a force of great social change. For those inside it, the key to retaining focus on the human is to be aware of the context in which you operate - and Cox can see all variations of the holistic approach.

"If you've got someone for an hour a week, play loads of football. Think of the kids as part of an ecosystem, where are they bouncing around, when are they going to play with their mates, play for your team, play for someone else's team, play other sports, going to the youth club, chase girls - they get a lot from those environments and that is really healthy. When you decide to be the main player in the ecosystem and we're going to ask you to be with us five days a week or we're going to take you out of school or be with you 15 hours a week... then you're starting to shape a childhood. You're a major source of information. You're going to shape the family life and decide when they can go on holiday and when they can't, what sports they might be able to play."

It is unclear whether some clubs do consider what it means to be a main player in the ecosystem. Given the nature of the well-documented 'race to the bottom' (professional clubs scouting at younger and younger ages), it seems questionable whether true consideration of the role they play in the dynamic entity that is a child's life has been made. Cox rightly points out that we might be heading towards the first generation of kids who have not played grassroots football because they arrived into the professional space so early. There are issues with this, evidently, but it also means football clubs must be even more aware of the role they play in young people's lives.

"That group of U9s I had at Watford, something like 33 percent of their waking childhood was shaped by me so if nothing else, you say to yourself this is a missed opportunity if I just focus on football here," Cox says. "I've got these kids in an environment where they are passionate, engaged, enthused. If I can use this to get more wins than just football, why wouldn't I?"

To do this you need the right people, and it's clear that Cox is that. More than his kind manner, engaging way of speaking and visible passion for his work, he has learned, after 20 years, to figure out how to put the person before the player.

In the Premier League, the Elite Player Performance Plan (EPPP) has been in place since 2012. This strategy is designed to create more homegrown players through a player-led approach. There are four steps, one of which is education, and in the EPPP statement the following is written:

"The Premier League aims to provide world-class education via inspirational and innovative teaching, which develops educationally rounded people through the delivery of a holistic approach... to support the technical, tactical, physical, mental, lifestyle and welfare development of all Academy players."

This kickstarted the idea for the fulltime training model from ages 12 through to 16 in the hope that moving the kids under one roof would give coaches more time with them. Cox was part of the first club, Watford, to set one up.

"I learned the hard way. If kids have Watford breakfast, get on a Watford bus to go to Watford school to hang out with boys who play for Watford and then train for Watford at night and then we do their homework with them at Watford, when you release them you haven't released them from an element of their life but you've basically said your whole identity that we created for you is now of no use to you."

One of Cox's favourite phrases is 'unintended consequences' and it was indeed exactly that that caused the holes in the EPPP's idea to appear. In fact, everything we do has unintended consequences. Coaching at a young age doesn't have to be problematic, but if it is tied to a professional association and the child gets a feeling they are being tested and assessed and that they might get released then that is clearly a bad but sometimes unintended consequence. If some clubs entice children into their programmes with rewards, then you create a situation where young children are receiving rewards for their ability, which is obviously a destructive consequence.

The key is to be flexible, not to think that one approach fits all (as was demonstrated in Sweden) and ultimately to make sure everyone is treated like the individual person they are.

"If you think about the teachers you had as a kid, the ones you thought were great, they made you feel special, right?" Cox asks, getting me thinking and nodding straight away. "They knew about you as a person and were invested in you and they might give you a bollocking but you'll take it because you can sense they like you. And then you had some other teachers who just wanted to teach you the subject. They didn't care about you as a person. One of those teachers is more skilled than the other and it's not different from football coaches."

With community work in the modern era and the way players engage with youth teams - as Cox mentioned earlier with the first team visiting the U12s museum - it is clear that some room for human development exists at the first team level. I believe much more could be done, but the pressure of the first team world leaves the focus on results and the coach with a constant fight on their hands.

"In a world where football has gone short term, managers are living six games ahead of themselves," Cox says. "I've just got to survive for six games, which involves winning. I'd love to do all that other stuff and I will do all that stuff, but I've just got to win these six games before I get round to that. I still need to win six games... I haven't got time."

Naturally Cox operates in a different world, one where he has time to care about the legacy of the person. The life of an academy manager is drastically different to the one of a first team manager. Where Cox's planning considers a 12-year journey, a head coach is working month to month. While Cox works with young people who are not yet professional and may never be, coaches are working with people receiving large sums of money who are already professional. As is the case with playing and coaching, the two are in the same industry but different professions.

The best head coaches, the ones who last the longest, they make sure that all forms of development never stop. As Cox says, “They’re invested in people, environment, culture, respect.” There’s no doubt that while not a first team head coach, Nick Cox is invested in all of those areas, and the children and staff working at Manchester United’s academy have benefited greatly from an approach that considers them people first, professionals second. Or as Cox himself likes to put it: “I’m a developer and my skill is sports science. That’s absolutely the way round it should be.”

5

Psychology

Perhaps those most responsible for human development in sporting organisations are sports psychologists. Often though, that work is hampered by the stigma that visiting one implies a fault or a failing. In truth there is so much to learn from the world of psychology, and indeed in recent years many athletes have spoken about working with psychologists to improve performance, but also aspects such as mental strength or confidence.

In such a well-researched and vast field, it is easy to get lost in ideas and papers. I spoke to clinical psychologists who work with athletes and coaches as well as a performance consultant to hear their thoughts on the development of the person. Their tales of professional experience resonated because all of their ideas and examples were rooted in looking after the person before the player. The definition of human development may well vary from person to person but all the conversations I had provided more understanding of how to connect, how to see a soul inside a person.

Stephen Rollnick is a professor of psychology who grew up in Cape Town but lives and works in Wales. Despite being co-founder of a revolutionary idea in psychology, he insists that it took him decades to see its wider relevance and how it might support what coaches and teachers were doing in their everyday practice.

In the early 1980s, Rollnick read William R Miller's paper on Motivational Interviewing (MI). Miller realised that in his work in addiction counselling the more he tried to instil wisdom into people, let alone judge or label their motivation, the more they would resist and protect themselves. The problem, Miller suggested, lay not in there being something wrong with the person in question, but in a counsellor-client relationship undermined by a confrontational style. This observation marked a key shift in the way addiction treatment was handled, and MI soon spread into diverse fields, spawning a vast body of research. For Miller, the key thing was to shift from instilling motivation to eliciting it from the person themselves.

Miller's background was in Rogerian therapy - an approach created by one of the most influential psychologists ever, Carl Rogers, in which the client takes an active role in the session because they know what is best. This inspired Miller to listen rather than confront and in doing so he noticed a willingness to change behaviour.

"Nobody had made the simple observation that the way you speak to someone will impact their motivation, how much they lie and deny, and whether or not they will change their behaviour," says Rollnick.

Having shared similar experiences and read and reviewed Miller's paper, Rollnick changed his practice. A few years later the pair coincidentally met in Sydney in neighbouring offices, which is where the ideas came from for what became a best-selling book. At the time, they thought it was for addiction psychologists then realised how widespread conversations about change were for people working in healthcare, criminal justice, schools and most recently, sport.

"Efforts by others to instil wisdom, change and growth in people through direct persuasion have their limits, and using the principles and skills in MI can produce some wonderful outcomes. People seem more able to take ownership of their own growth," Rollnick says.

Less instruction, more gentle guidance is the motto. The approach is not designed for people to just take liberties and run with how they want to change things but rather one of scaffolding the conversation about change to maximise progress.

"The inclination in many conversations about change is to take over the learning process," Rollnick says. "Driven by an attitude of 'I know what's best for you' people then use what I have called *the righting reflex* where they spot a problem and with the best of intentions and without giving it a second thought, set about solving it for the person."

There is a fine line between wanting to help someone, and inserting your own beliefs and experiences into a situation. It's natural and in many ways a reflex to use your own experience to help others, but we should spend more time really listening and guiding rather than talking and pointing.

The same is true in sport, which is part of the reason why MI can be so effective in this space. While confrontation and direct instruction are useful and necessary in many situations, there is a need to widen the skill set for helping people to improve.

"Where they are grappling with something inside them, doubt, uncertainty, hesitancy, that is where MI can help," Rollnick says. "Of course you can confront them and try to persuade them out of their hesitancy, but we believe if someone is ambivalent you'll get better outcomes by helping someone solve it for themselves."

He uses the example of a footballer whose position in the squad has changed. The player wants to get selected but they don't like the new position and have gone home agonising about it, unsure whether to go along with it to secure selection or to tell the coach about the positional issue.

"To have a conversation with someone like that you first have to understand how they think and feel, free of fear, which is all part of cementing a relationship," Rollnick says. "Even if it's for a few minutes, understand their experience. That makes them recognise this is a different kind of conversation. There's a lot of evidence outside of sport that this kind of listening improves outcomes."

Rollnick believes that sometimes listening and understanding might be all that is needed, which shows two things. One, that the smallest change in communication can have a big effect and two, that for too long we have not spent enough time listening and understanding if that can help people change the way they think about their situation. Rollnick says that in mental health, it's often not the treatment you offer but rather empathic listening that is the strongest predictor of good outcomes.

If more is needed than listening, Rollnick believes the style of a guide is appropriate. "Ask the person how they see the pros and cons of this new position they've been put into. Get out of their way while they hear themselves."

If they are guided towards talking about the positives of the new position, they might end up saying 'maybe I could do it' and for Rollnick, the maybe is an example of change talk. The simple acknowledgement of why change might be okay and how they might do it has a seismic impact on their mental state and willingness to change, and is far more effective than you telling them the same. Add follow-up conversations to this and the scaffolding is set and growth is in motion.

"This is not a holy grail or quick fix. It is not a technique you use on people but it's a way of being and speaking with them," Rollnick says.

Most coaches got into the job because they enjoy the opportunity to help people grow, which, as Rollnick points out, makes this approach far from new. "That part of their heart that wants to guide people into enjoying themselves, improving and becoming more skilful is the foundation for motivational interviewing."

In sport, getting coaches to be open enough to change from the rigid structures of the past is a challenge, and many players will likely have come out of the same system, expecting to be told what to do. If that is what they need, then that is what they need. Ultimately, the player will help you understand what they need. For Rollnick, coaches should consider the following:

"Work on your self and be reflective about the way you are and your relationships, and consider adopting this style of a guide and secondly, focus strongly on what the players feel will be helpful to them, and ask them."

Through the experiences of Rollnick and others, backed up by a considerable body of research, it is clear that MI is effective. Rollnick believes that the reason it hasn't made the widespread jump to sports coaching yet is that coaching education needs to do a better job of placing relationship-building skills close to the centre of their efforts.

A football coach at an elite club coaching a youth team has done just that. Speaking to Rollnick the coach has explored how he might help a group of players, not just one person, to take more decisions for themselves, even in high-octane situations like half-time team talks.

After recording the exchange and discussing it with Rollnick, the coach has seen dramatic improvement in this area. His approach has led him to having each of his players answer two questions - how they felt about the first half and how they would like to improve in the second. The players all hear each other talk about how they want to improve, the coach summarises this and then adds a few of his own observations.

By choosing to get his players to connect first, then have them share their experiences before finally giving his own dose of motivation, the coach has shown great strength in character. He has recognised that he doesn't have all the answers, but more than that he has also given his team the chance to take more control of what and how to change.

If there is one thing Rollnick knows how to navigate better than most, it is change. After years of working in addiction and healthcare, he is now also working in education and sport, helping coaches with their communication and reflectiveness, amongst other things. In one of our conversations, he talks to me about a young professional rugby player.

"He arrives late for practice so the chief coach later sends him a text asking him to give a two-minute presentation to his teammates about what it means to play for the club," Rollnick tells me, obviously keeping names out of it.

My initial reaction was 'what a great response.' It is giving the player the chance to learn from his mistake by expressing the importance of playing for the team, and in front of his teammates too. Stephen Rollnick does not agree and here is why.

"It's a form of punishment," Rollnick explains. "It's one of the major issues in sport I think, the traffic light system in a coach's brain - this idea of the coach being the deficit detective who spots what's wrong and tells others how to rectify things. If you're on the side of the field you'll be shouting a lot and your seniors will think you're quite good because you're saying 'no, communicate' as if that's going to help someone. As long as I'm emitting a rectification of deficits that's my job. With that frame in mind, they view behaviour in players - not people - as good or bad. They're looking to see if things are getting better or getting worse. This rugby coach saw something getting worse and like a traditional schoolteacher thought, 'I've got to point this out' and 'there must be consequences.' The consequence of bad behaviour here is: 'You're being punished, I've got to give a growth experience.'"

I realised I had fallen for the idea without considering the truth, which is that punishment is not a solution. Taking this road just makes people feel defensive and while they might conform, likely out of fear, it limits real growth. For that to happen, a simple conversation with them about why and how they might change is far more effective.

"Behavioural problems are opportunities for growth," Rollnick continues. "The direction of that growth is inside the person. I would sit down and talk to this young man. Before you know it, the guy is exploring inside himself - if he feels safe enough - his own good reasons to change."

Former surgeon and medical administrator Aidan Halligan once said: "You get your authority from how much you care." Halligan fought for better patient care by helping doctors to learn from their mistakes. He believed in a holistic approach. He was a great man and after listening to his lectures online and reading about his work, I was left wondering how many people are out there, in sport or in life, following a mantra of authority built from care? In sport, I couldn't help but think that not enough people do care.

Rollnick clearly does, and that is why his work is making a difference. He believes that while agreeing on things not to do, making small changes and sending people on courses are all well-intentioned, they are unlikely to make a change to culture. Indeed, as we saw in Denmark and in Sweden, if the entire club buys into this approach then culture can be changed. Everyone has to see themselves as a person for growth for it to become an evolving and living process.

If you don't have the person then you won't have the player, a concept Rollnick agrees with. "If you don't have their hearts, forget about their heads," he says. Ultimately he believes it comes back to leadership, that word that is so often used without really thinking about what it means.

If the leadership of an organisation really does believe in human development, then it will select coaches who are on a learning journey rather than just picking those who deliver results. It will, pivotally, assess how coaches view themselves rather than how they view players.

Time is always the issue, but not for Rollnick. "I think there's a paradox here. Taking a few moments to listen and guide a player saves time, because you are less likely to experience a repetition of the attitude or behaviour again. It's not time you're taking, it's progress you're making," he says. You are actually saving time by making time for human development.

I wonder how open high-performance sport is to really seeing who you are if who you are isn't going to help winning. If we don't accept people for who they are, then not only can we not help them create a space in which they might want to change but we also continue to create this image of sport as an experience that doesn't allow people to be accepted for who they are. This leads to the great question of identity.

One way to help human development take on a more integral role is by assessing identity. Who are you - a teammate, a partner, a child, a sibling? Each part of the person we are is on show at different times, but who you really are is the combination of those identities not the division of them.

"Ultimately the aim is to integrate, and the most healthy people are the ones who are the most integrated," says Dr. Suzanne Brown, a clinical psychologist working in performance, over a Zoom call towards the end of 2020. Brown, who used to work with Arsenal Women, is warm and even without being able to talk face-to-face, it is clear how passionate she is about her work and human development.

"People often talk about wearing the mask, not just in sport but throughout life," Brown says, discussing how the versions of ourselves that we present are in fact inauthentic.

"My experience has been helping shed those layers of defence which would obviously have been created for an important purpose at that time. If you think about being a six or seven-year-old, even alongside sport you've still got life happening, parental divorce, death. We build up these defences for the purpose of survival and often it's about those becoming really rigid and inflexible and changing our identity and it not being a true reflection of our true self."

While it may be helpful to separate identities for different occasions, such as sport and home for example, it is ultimately not healthy or sustainable. Compartmentalising might be effective in the short term, but it is still a form of hiding some element of who you really are. On top of that, it is exhausting.

Talking to Brown about human development through identity sees us discuss almost everything including early development, intergenerational experiences and how most of what we do is connected to unconscious processes. It's clear that for Brown, how we move around the world is determined by how we understand ourselves, our expectation of others and, as a result, what we expect from the world.

To do any of that, indeed to pursue any aspect of human development, you must want to do it. Once again, while I have written it before, it is worth repeating: For human development to be a part of an organisation's culture everyone must buy in. As Brown says: "In any high-performance culture, you essentially want everyone to see they have room for improvement."

Brown cites Kiwi psychologist and doctor, Ceri Evans, who is famous for the idea that everyone must not only recognise they have a gap in their development but must also be willing to close it. Some gaps may take no time at all to close, some longer, but all require regular and constant attention.

One of the great misconceptions of human development, especially with something like identity, is that it can be done in a session or two. Again, perhaps as a result of the quick-fix model that has exploded in recent years we are conditioned to believe this is possible. We want there to be solutions that we can understand, that are quick, but like anything complex it takes time to make lasting change.

Perhaps there is no bigger challenge than making personal development a priority, not just in sport but in society too. Why are we not teaching emotional awareness and intelligence in schools? The answer is likely connected to teachers burdened by rigid structures, endless examinations and a more business approach to education. Perhaps if we were able to review what we are teaching children today we might find space through recollections of history, literature or geography for areas such as emotional intelligence and conflict resolution to take a more prominent role. In doing so, we might be able to build a stronger foundations for young people as they go through the many and varied changes of adolescence.

"This is about early intervention, prevention better than cure," Brown says. "Helping children understand what they're feeling and how that relates to what they're doing is important."

Essentially we're talking about human relationships. It is one thing to hear about them, another to have them and something completely different to learn about them. Given that they are in many ways the lifeblood of our existence, shifting our focus seems not only logical but long overdue.

In high-performance sport, an outcome-based world, it is much harder to realign the focus on something other than the performance. Sport can, by definition, either be a physical activity done for enjoyment or a game or competition that requires physical effort and is done following rules. In today's language though, it is rare to hear the word sport used in a context that isn't connected to the latter. It can be no surprise then that even the amateur world is becoming increasingly impacted by outcomes. As I showed in *Mensch* through my adventures in amateur football in Germany, the line between enjoyment and competition at the lowest level has almost disappeared. While *Soul* is focussed on exploring the impacts of human development largely at the high-performance end of the sporting spectrum, it is intriguing that the space for enjoyment is becoming smaller and smaller as competition seeps into more and more aspects of our life.

In both sporting worlds we must pivot away from the

dominating lens of performance because ultimately, if the performance is the outcome then our life becomes one-dimensional, our identity restricted to just one space. Indeed, the same is true for many of us, whatever we do. We are more than the number of followers we have, sales we make, clicks our article gets, and while the need to reach professional standards obviously remains we must be wary not to be reduced to numbers and performance.

"In my experience working with the general public, it is desperately needed. We are a nation [UK] of terribly suppressed people," Brown says. "It isn't unique to sport but you do find at times quite a toxic environment in sport."

If we were willing to open up more of sport to human development, we might be able to remove some of that toxicity, which in turn might give other fields food for thought. Take sport's association with attachment and endings for example. Exploring this, as Brown has, can give us language and understanding to something so many of us experience but rarely put words to.

"There's such a lot of experience of endings in sport that I think really magnifies and creates a barrier in terms of people's willingness to engage," Brown says.

If people are not willing to engage then it is going to be hard to know what is driving them, although for Brown there are two fundamental drives. One is the need to connect and the other is the need to be autonomous and separate. As in every aspect of life though, balance is hard.

"People often say 'that really resonated with me' because people tend to sacrifice one for the other," Brown says. "It's very hard for us to be in that middle space. Either you sacrifice who you are and what you believe in to belong to the group or you sacrifice belonging to the group to just be separate, to have your own sense of who you are."

Add to that the reluctance many have with connecting to people who, in an industry of constant change, are not often in one place for very long and it is easy to see why a lot of sport is indeed dealing with attachment and ending.

In many ways, it is like being in love. People tend to be less wiling to be vulnerable if they have had their heart broken and often we are willing to sacrifice who we are just to be in a situation that we think is good for us. Given that it activates the same regions in the brain and both cause physical pain, the similarities are perhaps more striking than first considered. Human development may not have the same marketing as love, but it is worth the same amount of attention.

Just as having your heart broken is not only about love, it is equally unfair to place the blame for the lack of support for human development in sport at the feet of sport itself. It has its issues but there is also the other part of sport, the part we don't speak enough about - the joy of sport.

"Sport brings so much positive well-being and mental health to people but we tend to focus on the negative," Brown says. "But that's not the whole story. I continue to see people who maybe I did see when they were in crisis, but they've come through that crisis and they're thriving now and we continue to work together. It's important to let people know it doesn't have to end when you're no longer in that crisis. It's then about how can you maximise your potential, improving off the pitch just as much on the pitch."

Johan Cruyff's 'Total Football' was inspired by positional play and the use of triangles. With the help of assistant coach Tex Winter, legendary basketball coach Phil Jackson won 11 NBA Championships using the 'Triangle Offense.' Perhaps it's time sport invested in some different triangles, namely those designed by David Malan, a British psychotherapist.

Malan developed the triangle of conflict and the triangle of persons in the late 1970s to explore how your past unconsciously affects your present. Brown is inspired by this approach and believes exploring core emotions can reveal a great deal.

As shown in Individual Psychotherapy and the Science of Psychodynamics, 2Ed, Malan developed the triangle of conflict and the triangle of persons in the late 1970s (figure 1.).

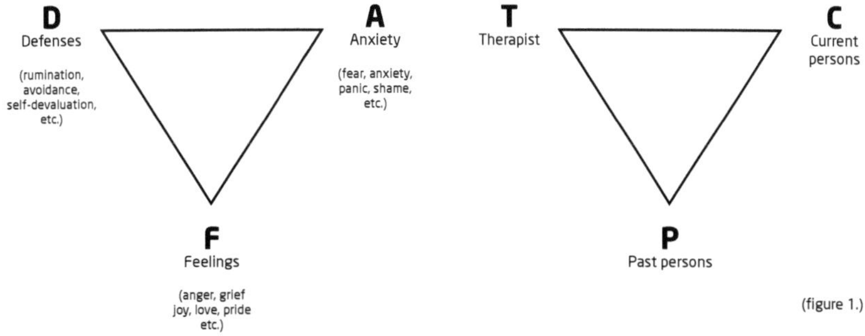

(figure 1.)

On the left is the triangle of conflict, where we deal with our own feelings and therefore what anxiety and defences this provokes. On the right is the triangle of person, referring to others. The P stands for past figures in your life, such as mother or father. The C represents the other people you relate to in this way, say a partner or a friend, and the T symbolises how those same feelings, anxieties and defences are activated with a therapist.

Malan's triangles are intriguing and worthy of discussion although in a high-performance scenario perhaps suffer from a lack of punch. Sadly this is a common issue for many scientific theories, as the abstract or overly intellectual nature of the theory prevents people from accessing it.

"In my experience, we really struggle with the complexity of whatever it may be in life," Brown says. "We just want it to be reduced, we want it to be simplified. Under pressure, on the pitch, 2-0 down, you haven't got the mental capacity to probably tolerate a lot of complexity, but actually outside of that how you work to help integration so that you've got clarity matters."

Sometimes using something familiar can make something new less intimidating. If you pass and move using the triangle you are more likely to create scoring opportunities. Consider then that if you pass and move your feelings around with the right person you are more likely to create opportunities for increased understanding and growth. In an appropriate context, even difficult subjects can be made accessible.

Nevertheless, all work must contend with the limits of individuals and ignorance of structures. Brown knows that for all her knowledge and skill, she, like every therapist, psychologist or anyone working in human development, is not omnipotent. None of us has all the answers and to pretend otherwise would not only be foolish but also dangerous. Ultimately, there are also some things that only we ourselves can change.

"If people are attached to suffering or some element of self-sabotage - I don't have a way through that. If you're the architect of this wall then only you can bring it down," Brown says. There are of course ways in which to help people feel more equipped to take down any proverbial wall in their mind, but the actual act of doing so is very much theirs to make."

Even then, an individual's decision to make a change might be hindered by the structure in which they exist. The structure of many high-performance sports, especially football, is pathway-driven, with an obsession about processes. This somewhat military experience is contradictory to human nature, and indeed human development.

"Human beings don't like to be told what to do, so actually when you start to give them choice that's a revelation for them. They're not used to it but it speaks to their inner drive of wanting to be the author of their own life," Brown says.

You can tell people what to do, but it will not be as effective as extending your hand and offering a way to do things differently. As Rollnick mentioned earlier: less instruction, more guidance.

To do this effectively you need to find the right people. If you're looking to bring people in full time then it's important they share and embody the values of the organisation. Most importantly you need people who can connect. While both people in this scenario will be learning together, it is pivotal that the guides, the Gandalfs of this world, are qualified. As Brown notes, "If you were having an operation you'd want the surgeon to know exactly where they needed to go rather than hack you up to find something."

Why is this all important? Because people are people no matter what profession they chose. We all need help to understand our past, what we're feeling in the present and how to understand who we are. Brown says she has worked with people who have won Olympic medals but came out of their career needing deep work. After all, the medal weighs differently when you're not on the podium.

What does that gold medal mean? In a sporting sense it means the ultimate achievement. Opportunities, greater expectations, greater reward - much will change as might you but life itself remains the same. Substitute gold medal for any sporting achievement and the same is true. It means something, absolutely. It matters, no question. But your life is still built around the same foundation of being physically and mentally healthy and the people in your life. If you weren't happy before you won gold, you won't be happy after.

These ideas were expressed by Rick Cotgreave as we chatted over a video call, a form of interaction that quickly became the norm during the pandemic. Despite the lack of human contact and the increased screen time, remote conversations with people throughout the majority of *Soul* were still a great source of comfort, enjoyment and inspiration.

Cotgreave is a former PE teacher and England lacrosse player with over 20 years of coaching experience in the field. He now works as a performance coach and consultant in the business world, as well as helping athletes transition out of sport.

When I ask about his view of human development, it is telling that we start with the Sanskrit word Samtosa - the deliberate act of contentment. Cotgreave realised when he gave up lacrosse, did more climbing and yoga, where he came across the word, that there is a misconception about mediocrity and stagnation in sport and in life. He started to be grateful for more and realised that while the dopamine satisfaction of progress continues to be a powerful drug in sports, the serotonin we need from connection and relationships is just as valuable. Not everything had to be about winning or improvement.

Herein lies sport's greatest battle, though. While those playing sport for the sake of enjoyment tend to avoid this issue because their motivation to play is not connected to improvement, those competing in high-performance sport are faced with the conundrum: can they be content in the face of never-ending progress?

"Sport is predicated on dissatisfaction," Cotgreave tells me. "You've got a personal best but it's only there to be beaten. You've made an England team, now you need to be in the starting line-up. There's never enough. Sport, society, academia - they are all built into that."

What is the message of living in a world where everything we do is never enough? Other than being exhausting, it means constantly living in a place that is dissatisfied. Journalism is terrible for this - riting for one outlet is just a step to writing for the next. Similarly, getting more followers on social media is a never-ending process. You are always told to strive for something bigger, always judged by your last big byline. It is hard to take the perspective that what you might have already achieved is in fact great, wonderful, brilliant - unless you deliberately choose otherwise.

"I can get seduced by the ambition that better never stops," Cotgreave says. As he says this I am reminded of Germany's national team motto once being "the best never rest". Other than this not being true - rest is an integral part of the best athletes' recovery - it is a further example of the carrot of progress being dangled at every opportunity. It is all-encompassing. The problem with that is that progress eventually becomes how you measure your own self-worth.

"The flip side of 'I need to be better tomorrow' is that it doesn't take much to say 'I'm not good enough today' - and that's not healthy," Cotgreave says, poignantly.

Part of this issue is the growth model, the idea that for every step of everybody's professional lives we must be looking to get better. While development is important, it is also necessary to remind ourselves of what we have done and what we have. It's not always about the next game, goal, byline, promotion or wage level. The knock-on effect of this model is that too many people feel they haven't yet achieved enough. I think we need to remind ourselves and each other that there is great value in serving a community, a small group, a family. It is great to aspire and work towards more but it is equally important that we remember not getting there is not a problem or a failure. People make an impact every day all over the world. Just because they're not a professional athlete, insanely wealthy or have a million followers on Instagram doesn't mean that isn't significant. I think we need to remember that because too often we are told to forget it.

Perhaps the death knell for the premise of this book though, is how much of developing the person is on sport? Clearly, not all of it, perhaps not even as much as I thought. Sport is there to entertain, to make money, to provide opportunity to thousands, but with that comes exposure, expectation and financial reward. For those reasons alone, it must play a much greater part of the process than it already does. It has a duty, a responsibility to do more.

Changing club or association culture is one way to effectively implement human development, but to make an impact in altering the system means taking a look at the bigger picture. Too much of sport is designed to commodify the athlete, a phrase Cotgreave credits as originating from Ian Braid, the former CEO of the British Athletes Commission (BAC) and the founder of the DOCIAsport (Duty of Care In Action) consultancy. The capitalist system turns people into objects of trade. It removes their humanness, but in exchange it offers you a chance to play sport on the big stage and become a hero to a community.

"There is a problem with the willingness of the athlete to be commodified as well as sport commodifying it," Cotgreave says.

Early specialisation is a great example of this. The encouraging examples such as AIK are few and far between. The majority of the major sports do not operate according to this system and because children want to compete, play in the Premier League, win Super Bowls, they specialise. They play the game because they want the chance to win, and the game knows this.

"I think kids know going into an academy early on there's going to be a sacrifice to normal life, whatever that might be," Cotgreave says. "If that means you lose the friends you had growing up, then you'll have a new group in sport. There's a social cost, but that's more than made up because you have teammates. There might be a physical cost because coaches might work you really hard, which brings a higher risk of injury, perhaps even attritional injury as well. You accept that risk as well. Career-wise, it's probably going to take you out of your education so you can focus on sport. Academically, you're going to fall behind your peers but you're not told to worry because you're developing another skill set. Again, you make that trade. While your mates are 21, 22, 23 and getting jobs you're still chasing a football and believing that's important but you carry on doing that. Yes, you can make big money but in terms of a career you'll still be a player while they become a manager or a leader in a business. Again, you're probably willing to make that sacrifice. All of that is quite explicit. I think what we're not talking about is to pursue this sport to the level you are doing is going to be a sacrifice on your overall human development. Is your mental well-being going to be jeopardised as a result of entering this sport? I think so. How you define your success becomes one-dimensional. You're going to be kept hungry, winning isn't enough, you need a legacy. Are we as explicit in terms of the mental health cost of entering this sport?"

There are of course differences between individual and team sports, but taking the aforementioned example, if you end up accepting all of those risks and successfully beat thousands of others to the spot you're in, what has that cost you? Athletes are not only often forced into systems and structures that do not consider the holistic angle but also encourage them to commit behaviours that outside of sport would be deemed concerning. Inside sport though, it is deemed as a necessary part of the sacrifice to achieve the dream. That is not to say that hard work and skill development are not necessary, but the pursuit of technical perfection through obsessive behaviour is not healthy.

In 2013, Nike released an advert with Tiger Woods accompanied by the words: "Winning takes care of everything." This was something Woods himself said, but in both cases it reiterates the idea that if you win in the field of sport then the rest of your life will be fine. This is a dangerous message to send, and as Woods' case proved is certainly not true.

If the testimonies offered in the 2021 Tiger Woods documentary *Tiger* are to be believed, then it is clear that Woods missed out on an enormous part of human development in exchange for golfing excellence. After shame, injuries and rehabilitation, Woods finally got around to realising he needed to work on himself, his emotions, in essence his humanness. That he would return in 2019 to win his 15th major championship was remarkable, but also proof that we can win as humans, that we needn't channel a machine-like approach in order to be successful. We needn't pay such a high price.

Cotgreave is working to address that cost. "How can I help shift the narrative and a belief pattern that has created success in sport to help create fulfilment in life? Can I shift the idea of progress and never-ending more and more to the idea of you are good enough?"

Part of that is connected to sports psychology, something that Cotgreave believes can actually be counterproductive if done incorrectly. "I think the danger of sports psychology is that it keeps people hungry," Cotgreave says.

"What I'm talking about is maintaining energy – hunger represents a deficit or a level of dissatisfaction – we eat to satisfy a need or demand. If the demand is removed then so is the energy to meet it. To keep us hungry for success we need to be dissatisfied with what we have. Psychologists can be skilful in leaning into the natural hedonic adaptation and pushing athletes to want more and more, keeping them chasing personal bests and medals."

Therapy though, that makes well-rounded human beings. They don't only have a performance lens, as Cotgreave explains, which means they are able to allow the entire personal development to become a priority.

"It's in this realm that contentment, satisfaction with what we have, appreciation and gratitude can come into play. Therapy makes well-rounded human beings, but if athletes made it to therapy their career would effectively be over. Not because of perception but because the therapist would ask: 'Why are you doing something that is causing you angst, depression, and having you follow a ridiculous food regime?' We need to solve that but with the narrative of winning the medal still there. You can't."

Cotgreave recently experienced this himself when he competed in a swimming race, something he does regularly but wasn't able to do much of lately because of the pandemic. In a recent competition he finished second and his first thought was not, 'Rick, you're 50, you finished second in a race of 250 people and what a great day out it was' but rather 'I didn't win.'

So how to strike the balance of progress? The latter can obviously be beneficial, but how often do we remind ourselves that sometimes we can and should look to find contentment in what we already have, largely because it is often so much more than we think.

"There is truth that happiness can come from progress towards your goals, which sport is very good at, but there is also truth that happiness comes from contentment and acceptance and gratitude. So how can both be true?" Cotgreave asks. "There is a balance to be found between recognising that too much contentment can lead to mediocrity and boredom and that too much trusting of the process can lead to burnout and stress. "

"The only thing I came up with is the 45 degree angle that says, this is where we play and thrive."

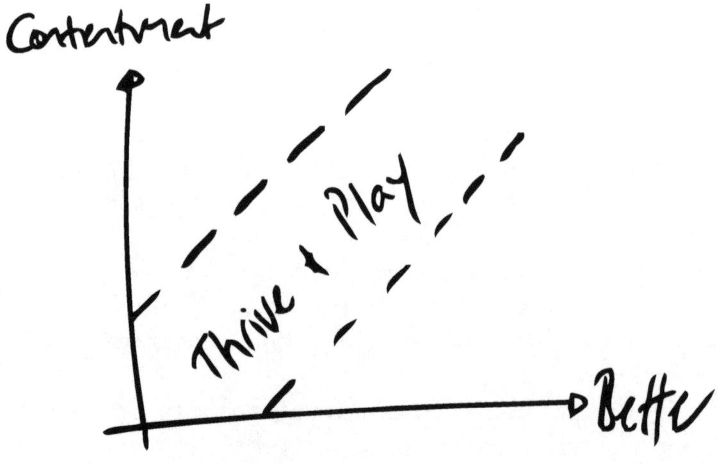

"So the first time you go and kick a football you're a bit crap at it but because you enjoyed it you came back. What happens in sport is that someone comes along and says, 'Come on Jonathan you could be good at this if you trained' and then we pull you from the diagonal and put you in the side called better and then the world is only about progress, it forgets the enjoyment bit. So the bigger question, what's human development? Ultimately it's to reintroduce the idea of thriving and playing because then at least that way you can have both progress and enjoyment."

This concept is not unheard of in high-performance sport either, where you often hear athletes talk about how much their performance is connected to their enjoyment. This battle all starts at school though, and as a former physical education teacher Cotgreave knows this all too well.

"Why do we have PE on the curriculum and who do I need to pick for the first cricket or basketball team? Am I about performance or participation? If it's participation then we are talking about a kid who is more well-rounded, more capable of forming relationships and recognising the value of losing and not getting selected. But if you've got a kid on a performance angle then I think with a lot of the development work around more balance and self-awareness, the only lever you've got is to say: 'This is going to help you perform.' You end up doing this peculiar version of self-development which is actually only about performance."

Much like AIK's academy made first-team players the byproduct of their approach rather than the focus, performance should be the byproduct of helping children to be more well-rounded rather than the reason. At the high-performance level, the emphasis and expectation on performance is so great that development beyond contributing to performance is rarely considered. Winning is what matters. Winning every day, session, game or competition. And once you've done that, you do it again.

I wonder how can we expect anyone to perform if we have not looked after who they are first? Furthermore, I wonder about the real significance of winning. In competition, in sport, the concept of winning is necessary. It is what gives stakes to what we watch. It is why sporting contests are spectacles. There is great value in the idea of winning, both in striving for and viewing of it. The clarity, albeit sometimes crushing if you're on the wrong side of the result, that competition brings is useful. It mirrors life's gains and losses, but it doesn't mirror all of life. There is much more to and in life that lands in the grey area, that is not quantifiable by the metric of win or loss. That is the key difference.

"Unfortunately sport can only be about winning," Cotgreave believes. "But life cannot only be about winning because by definition only one person can do it. It's a zero sum game that leaves us nowhere for second place."

So what do we want? What does sport want? It's a question that perhaps doesn't have an answer. What is clear though, to aim for more well-rounded individuals with a grasp on their emotions, capable of compassion and empathy, equipped to engage in healthy debate, and aware of their character traits is an admirable and desirable goal for obvious reasons. But does that too have a price?

"How many well-rounded champions do you know?" Cotgreave asks me. I admit, I had to pause. To return to the aforementioned example of Tiger Woods, does he dominate as much as he did without detaching from his humanness? Maybe not, but that's partly because sport, and indeed much of life, has created this idea that if you do more than everyone else you will go further. Again there is a very fine line to be taken here because progress is of course valuable and indeed necessary, but it is the price it costs that needs further consideration. Woods might have won fewer majors in his career had he worked on his human development sooner, but he might have been better equipped to handle far more of his life as a result. The game of golf might have suffered, but maybe fewer people, Woods included, wouldn't have and that matters more.

Cotgreave believes that not only would we not have a Premier League if we had a world full of well-rounded people, but that without that variety of character the world would have stagnated. The movers and shakers of the world tend not to be well-rounded, Cotgreave believes. They are, like the athlete winning the 100-metre dash, the one percent of the one percent, the exceptional. They are the ones who make change. Perhaps that is true, but if it is are we asking enough questions about those heroes for the next generation? Furthermore, what does that mean for everyone who is well-rounded? Do those people not contribute to the balance of their communities and in doing so, make a change to the world?

There is no denying that sport is doing great things, and that it is such a great tool for so many, but the truth emerging more clearly with every conversation I have, one I had hoped wouldn't be true but is now undeniable, is that high-performance, top-level sport is consciously not doing enough to develop human beings unless it helps contribute towards performing, winning and/or business. To fight against that triangle is to lose. It would be man versus machine. But to turn that triangle into a square by adding space for human development is possible, and with every person I speak to I can see that there are many out there fighting for that to become a more tangible reality.

•

6

Well-being

By definition any concept with the word 'care' in it implies a certain degree of consideration for the human and so the emergence of player care in football in recent years was intriguing. Was this a similar role to character development just under a different name, or was it a job designed to cater for a footballer's every need? After chatting to Hugo Scheckter, the former head of Player Care at West Ham and now the man in charge of The Player Care Group, it was clear how much of a difference there was between the reality of the role and the perception of it.

"One of the criticisms I get a lot is you haven't shown the player how to do this, when they leave they won't be able to do this. You're doing everything for them," Scheckter tells me over a virtual call, a method of communication always accompanied by the pang that human contact is still beyond reach during the pandemic.

"You have to understand what type of player it is. Some players are never going to sit on the phone with a local council and set up a direct debit, never in a million years. I could say we're going to do a training session on it and the player will just tell me where to go and walk out. But it has to be done and if he doesn't care and doesn't want to do it, he's an adult, I'm not going to sit him down and say he won't play on the weekend because the coach isn't going to enforce that either. Sometimes you just have to get things done."

Indeed this is the major criticism I have heard from some coaches, as was the case with the academy coach in Germany I spoke to in chapter three, where he discussed his concerns with the role without naming it specifically.

"Clubs do appoint people to cater to the needs of the player but again there is a balance to be reached. If you take away too much responsibility from the players in order to avoid pitfalls and problems, then essentially all you do is cover up potential cracks in the player's character development... If we get the balance wrong we need to ask ourselves, what kind of person are we creating long term?"

The posing of that question feels valid, but is it the player care department that should be answering it?

"In an ideal world we are educating players on life lessons, but football needs results now," Scheckter explains. "We have a duty of care but we are not a school, we are not an education platform. Things need to get done and distractions away from football need to be taken away."

It is easy to suggest that every opportunity be used to develop character, but in very few cases is the player interested. The reality, as Scheckter outlines, is often very different and in a results-based environment that is not particularly surprising.

"In reality, football is a results driven world, the coach could be one game from the sack and if the star player is in prison because he was driving without a licence because he didn't realise non-EU citizens have to transfer their licence after a year then the coach will be asking questions not saying: 'Well, you've taught him a really good life lesson.'"

Ironically, were the job to spill more into that field Scheckter would be perfectly suited for it. He's a self-made man who loves sport and ventured to America to find a path when he initially wasn't able to forge one in the UK. He is a man who has spent most of his life getting things done, whether for himself or for others. He has spent his life dealing and helping endless personalities. He has already lived a lot of life and that helps him know what player care should, should not and cannot be. More often than not, the job demands pragmatism.

"A basic example would be a player doesn't pay their council tax, it goes to the bailiffs and on the morning of a match they show up on the door and start repossessing things. His wife is at home and doesn't speak English and calls the player and they're lost for the game," Scheckter explains, before telling me this actually happened to him once.

From a performance standpoint, this is obviously a disaster. "We're paying him 60, 70, 80 grand a week, whatever it is and I think he played in the game, but his head was gone which means we lost out on 80 grand's worth of player that week, and the points we may have missed."

Indeed, Scheckter rightly points out that player care is not a question of can clubs afford to do this but rather can they afford not to? In the *European Journal for Sport and Society*, Richard Elliott wrote a paper entitled "The man who would be worth billions: Vincent Pericard, migration and mental illness" in which he explains how important a club's environment can be on the mental health of a player. While a lot of Pericard's situation was about a lack of control and operating in a macho culture that did not welcome openness in terms of emotions, it also appears clear that had Portsmouth had player care at that time then Pericard's experience might have been different.

And this is where player care can and often does make an enormous difference. While player care might rarely be directly about human development, it remains intrinsically connected to it. It requires pragmatism, a good sense of judgement and great communication so as to put the right people together at the right time. Scheckter broadly defines the role as "everything that is not football or medical to do with a player at the club."

Sadly, too many take this as an invitation to interpret the role as primarily operational. Perception is part of the issue, as Scheckter was finding when we spoke. His newly founded consultancy is aimed at helping clubs either create a player care programme or improve their existing one, but Scheckter was often facing the fact people thought he was offering concierge work. That there is a misunderstanding in football about what player care is let alone what good player care looks like is troubling, but given the complexity and nuance of the job done properly perhaps not surprising. Ultimately, it appears football's focus remains on the efficiency, the numbers, the "what can we get done with this role" perspective. That focus is wrong.

The operational aspect is actually the easier aspect to the job, Scheckter explains. For example, if a player wants a car, the club has a good supplier, you send the player the brochure, they pick one and it gets delivered. The far more complex part is the relationship building. The operational aspect of the job will and has led to player care being dismissed as little more than a concierge role, but the real human development comes in the other half of the job.

"If something is important to a player then it needs to be important to me as well," Scheckter says, diligently. "Rather than always saying what is the most efficient way to do something you kind of want to be inefficient in order to foster a better relationship. For example, if a player's wife said to me 'I need curtains for the flat' I could easily say there's a guy coming over tomorrow to install them and done. But I might say 'Let's pop to the store and look through the fabrics and sort it together.' Then I have half a day where I am building a relationship with the wife and during that time she might tell me about how worried she is about her son, that he has learning difficulties and that she doesn't know if he's being looked after properly. Now, she never would have called me up to say that but in that inefficiency you've built that relationship. So while on paper it says you've taken eight hours to get curtains in reality you've got to a deeper part of the problem, got a better relationship and potentially solved a major issue they probably wouldn't have otherwise talked about."

To get here though, you need to have built up trust and respect, and have the required social skills to be able to navigate such conversations. Those working in player care have likely had the chance to make leaps and bounds with their own human development based simply on the number and variation of interactions they have to contend with. The result of that is the ability to create connection and build trust, as Scheckter has done in his career.

With that comes confidence and internal support. "I've never had a problem pulling a player to one side and saying 'Don't speak to me like that' or 'You were out of order then' and the club backs me," Scheckter says of a backing that is pivotal but takes a long time to earn. Early on in his career he was having to justify his work far too often, with the concept of player care already being put in a box and misunderstood.

"I was having to explain that my job is relationship based so me grabbing a coffee with someone can be really advantageous rather than me just sat at my computer just typing," Scheckter said, saying fighting off micromanagement can be one of the battles player care departments face.

The rigid, inflexible structures Scheckter describes might be from his past but they remain an issue in the present. Clearly, working in player care doesn't mean you are just someone who is good at talking or who will answer the phone every hour of the day. The job is about getting things done, but it is also about cultivating and managing relationships - which is a skill in itself. Sport, particularly football, needs to recognise the value of that rather than see it as a threat to power.

"It's about the relationships and knowing that if you call me at three in the morning it'll be an emergency and I will deal with it effectively because I will know your situation, who you are, and your level of English because I have that relationship with you," Scheckter explains.

The real trick, and ultimately what Scheckter believes to be the finest line to tread is simultaneously keeping the players, their families and the club happy. "Is a popular player care officer a good one? If they're a yes man then they'll be popular with the players but probably not with the club... It's hard to say what good player care looks like. You've got to be supportive of the club, the manager, as well as the players and their families. It's a strange role sometimes."

If you don't get the balance right, then players can think you unapproachable, and while the care you're aiming for would likely still be within reach, the building of strong relationships that might impact human development would not. The best kind of player care is the one in which people demonstrate empathic care.

Sadly too many clubs still believe that the higher the financial reward, the happier players must be. They're not willing to recognise that a player care department is not only not an expensive outlay, but may in fact save them money in the long run. As Rollnick said in chapter five: "It's not time you're taking, it's progress you're making."

And yet, many football clubs continue to see progress only through the prism of player development. Scheckter tells me in the last few months he has been blown away by conversations with some massive Champions League clubs about the lack of attention to detail and lack of personal approach. He recalls that one club told him when a player signed all they handed him was an A4 page printout of information.

Much like in life, the small things can make the biggest impact. That first day in a new job, at university or at the new club you've just signed for - those feelings of wanting to be of value and valued are the same throughout life. How you feel when you arrive in a new place will set the tone for how you behave in that space, how much you want to invest and what impression you have of how that organisation considers you as a person.

When working at West Ham, Scheckter's team created a personal, leather-bound welcome pack with information about everyone at the club, housing, schools, banking, transport, food, training ground details and stadium. It was translated into the player's language and every person's name (and a nickname if appropriate) was accompanied by a picture so that players could identify them. It appears a small act (astoundingly such items are not commonplace), and while Scheckter is aware that most will not read it cover to cover it is the feeling it provides that counts most.

"Small things lead to the big things," Scheckter says. "You can pay someone money but when you earn over a certain amount it's not your drive. At that level of footballer you're looking at the non-financial side of things to get them excited, such as a welcome pack or kits with kids' names on it when they arrive. You're talking about 100 pounds here but a bit of thought and effort makes a huge impact."

While the need for pragmatism means that genuine moments of human development are reduced, sometimes it is that pragmatism that can make all the difference for those footballers and their families who just need help. Furthermore, the relationships forged through good player care can lead to character development as two people learn about one another and how they might help each other. Good player care can be the difference between someone opening the door to a problem and not even realising there was one to walk through.

Perhaps that is player care's greatest secret - it works behind the scenes, allowing football to continue without having to acknowledge it. The pragmatic necessity of player care explains a great deal of how football sees itself. That Scheckter and many others recognise the need to get things done to make sure both the player's and the team's performance is not negatively affected is totally understandable. That football has not done more to make their job lean less towards the operational and more towards the relationship cultivating says a lot about football's understanding of player care and its unhealthy obsession with making performance the sole focus. Football might feel like it is played in a vacuum, especially during the pandemic, but footballers don't play football in a vacuum. They are human beings who need to be able to deal with life outside of the sport if they are to develop as people let alone find deep levels of joy later on in life.

"Footballers are paid an awful lot of money to almost sacrifice a lot of the human side of them," Scheckter says, poignantly. "They don't get time off, they don't get paternity leave, they don't get to go to weddings, they can get pushed, repeatedly injured at work. That's their work then that's fine and someone else will take their place."

Considering Cotgreave's words from chapter five in addition to all that Scheckter has said, the evidence continues to suggest that the reality of professional football is not the same as the dream it is sold as. The opportunity to be a hero to millions, be paid a fortune, have social power comes at a price. It costs them part of their humanness. Perhaps there is no changing the world in which prices are so readily paid, but there might be a way to lower the cost.

Steve Johnson is the CEO of the Well-being Science Institute in Australia, and runs the world's first recognised government accredited training programme for elite athlete well-being. He believes well-being will be to sport what strength and conditioning was 30 years ago. The shift to the person-then-player perspective is coming, and it starts with well-being.

Most definitions of well-being are centred around happiness or finding a sense of meaning and purpose. Happiness however can be fleeting, and is often tied to external factors. The greater, deeper emotion, the one we should turn our attention to, is joy. And reaching that is more likely if we take care of our well-being. Finding something we are passionate about is important but so too are other aspects of our lives.

Johnson's definition of well-being speaks to actively engaging in the areas of our lives that provide us with a great sense of meaning and purpose while also making us happy and giving us a sense of accomplishment through the achievement of goals and plans. For him and his team, well-being is defined as: "To move to your whole-person potential and live your life in a valued way."

It taps into something we all want, namely that sense of value. We all want to matter, on varying scales. We all want to feel like we are making a difference with our lives. In order to do that we must first understand not only what it is we value but how we make our life reflect those values. In doing so, we are more likely to be at peace with ourselves and indeed live our lives in a more valued way.

Considering the well-being of the people in your organisation is an integral part of any human development. For Johnson, the two are intrinsically connected.

"Well-being is human development," Johnson tells me over a video call in early 2021 in a calm, steady voice that conveys a depth of knowledge. "And central to human development is having self-awareness, personal growth initiative and focus in those areas of growth that you're interested in, that are aligned with your values and character and that enable your capacity to move to whole your potential. Mostly, athletes are encouraged by very short-sighted coaches to be unidimensional in their self-perception and in their well-being, and that has consequences for short, medium, and long term."

Johnson has never been short-sighted in his career. In fact, the origins of this idea took shape a good 27 years ago, when Johnson was a university lecturer in sport psychology. He made a connection through one of his students to a professional sports team in Australia, helping the team in areas he thought they were lacking. Remarkably they ended up winning the professional competition they were playing in. At the end of the season, Johnson was asked back and effectively designed a holistic approach to player well-being. The team loved the idea but told Johnson they weren't in a position to put it into place. Twenty-two years later, Johnson combined his idea with the technology of the modern era and created a holistic well-being app. Again, he was told the team wasn't ready, but this time they asked him to look at the club's well-being setup. Thirty-one recommendations later, Steve's idea finally began to take root.

After developing a training programme of 21 modules built around the principles of holistic well-being, positive psychology, self-determination theory (SDT), and solution-focussed coaching, Steve applied the well-being programme to an elite sporting context, added a suite of tools and to date has trained over 250 people working in well-being in Australian elite sport. Not done yet, Steve got this approved as a qualification by the Australian Government and he has also created a link with Loughborough University in the UK that has allowed him to help even more people around the world.

It is remarkable that even at the time we spoke in early 2021, Johnson's programme in Australia was still the only holistic well-being programme in the world. For all the money in sport, so little of it has been invested in the human being. Change is on the way though.

"From a player care perspective, sport is a long way back," Johnson says. "There is a continuum which starts with safeguarding that moves to welfare and player care and then well-being. My observation of what is in elite sport is that there is huge opportunity for improvement. Much of what is happening is very reactive, not holistic and very much a separation between performance and the player care field. Player well-being is yet to get a seat at the table in most organisations."

In Australia, well-being has its own table. Two athletes who were students on Johnson's well-being course ended up developing a well-being assessment tool for use in primary schools using language and emojis. The screening tool is now in 600 schools around Australia, and costs around five dollars per child. When children complete the screening tool, if anything gets flagged, an email is sent directly to the principal and he or she can take action immediately.

In sport, the Australian Rugby League leads the way when it comes to well-being. While European football might still be fascinated by those working in analytics, and the surface pads of the NFL hold much intrigue, there is a new department coming and it sounds very different.

"Rugby League in Australia is the world leader in holistic well-being, by a long way," Johnson tells me. "The National Rugby League has put its money where its mouth is. It has a proactive and developmental well-being strategy, has funded two full time qualified well-being managers per club (there are 16 clubs in the national competition) and provides all players with the opportunity to have a holistic well-being plan developed in conjunction with their well-being manager. In addition, players receive an annual study allowance of several thousand dollars, which they can apply to any area of interest.

Johnson believes it is relatively simple for other sporting codes to emulate what the NRL has done, mainly by first considering changing perspective on well-being. The biggest assets you have are on the field, court or in the arena, so doesn't it make sense that you help them as a person so they feel like their life is going well? If you combine that with a great organisational culture and great team culture, then you give that person the best chance of reaching their best potential in many of aspects of their life."

Ultimately, the real question is who is the person in the sporting organisation that plays that role? Intriguingly enough, it is unlikely to be the sports psychologist.

"Look at the history of psychology and the way in which psychologists get trained. In most countries around the world you can get a psychology degree and know very little about the body," Johnson says, opening a long-discussed can of worms in the field that dates back hundreds of years.

In the 17th century, philosopher René Descartes introduced

the idea of Dualism, which is basically the idea that the mind and the body are separate from one another, performing different functions albeit intertwined. Clearly today, psychology discusses this with a critical stance but the distinction between mind and body is still an enormous talking point.

"Psychology and mental health particularly today for many people still happens from the head up," Johnson says. "Yet even psychologists are now starting to say to people you need to eat, exercise and sleep well. But what's their training or qualification for those recommendations? Mostly they have very little training in these areas."

While some sports psychologists might have kept themselves ahead of the curve, many are bound by the context in which they work. As Rick Cotgreave discussed in chapter five, the idea of sports psychologists, even if well-intentioned, contributing to never-ending development can be problematic. The reasons for that are simpler than they first appear.

"The question we often need to ask is how does a sports psychologist get paid? Often they're paid by the coaching staff, which means their job is to maximise performance," Johnson points out, astutely. "If you don't perform, it's pretty clear from the coaching staff's perspective that you haven't done your job."

That is why Johnson's idea for a well-being manager makes so much sense, not only because they are focussed on the person outside of their performance (although not ignoring its effect on them as an individual) but also because they should report to the CEO of the organisation.

"In an ideal world, the well-being manager reports to the CEO because as we know the coach is always on the way to being fired. Even if you were to think of your athletes or your players being considered as an organisational asset, you want the CEO and the incoming coach to say 'this is the way we look after people at this organisation,' which is an employment value proposition, so it's an attraction tool, an engagement tool and it's a retention tool."

Reporting to the man at the top of the organisation is a masterstroke because, if done correctly, it not only allows for well-being to be sustainable but it also sets the tone for the entire organisation. Beyond the business language at the end of Johnson's reasoning lies further wisdom. If you value the people who work for you as a people then your business becomes more attractive, you can connect with your employees more and they are more likely to continue to work for you. Even outside of sport, this approach makes a lot of sense. One small action can make an enormous difference. Gone are the days of punching in and out. There is a different understanding in the world now.

"When it comes to decisions about contracts, being a well-being focussed organisation can make all the difference between whether someone stays or goes. If someone is offering you equal money or even a little bit more do you really want to go when the current organisation takes care of you and values you as a person and positively contributes to your family and your community? If the organisation says by its actions that they value you and your whole life it sends a clear message that they care about you as a person and you are far more likely to stay rather than go somewhere for a bigger cheque but not much else."

Those words hit hard - your whole life. The uttering of them in this context shows an appreciation for the concept, which is unlikely to be the case for most sports organisations around the world. Imagine though, for a moment, a sports team or company were to approach you with genuine consideration for how the rest of your life might run - and then backed it up with tangible action throughout your time working in that space. We know from family and friendships just how much that matters, how much we need that. Imagine what it would do to our well-being, to our souls, if our professional lives attempted to do the same.

"The well-being manager can separate from the coaching staff and truly put this whole person's needs at the centre and help them regardless of what the performance is, in the hope you can help the individual in a confidential way where your agenda is not just to maximise performance on the field. In a sense, you're actually on the athlete's side," Johnson says, perhaps revealing a startling idea that for too long organisations have not really been on the athlete's side.

Other than the need for a well-being department for modern sporting organisations, Johnson also believes that organisational development specialists who explain how organisations can improve strategically in terms of capability, functioning and process, are also going to be in demand in the years ahead. Given that Johnson used to work in corporate consulting and was "sucked into the management vortex" he knows all about organisational change.

It is clear speaking to Johnson that for well-being to work, you have to start by recognising you will need a change plan and it will have to be specific. Change is complex and simplifying it rarely brings much success. You have to consider each part of the change. From players to coaches, CEOs to the club as a whole, each approach requires a different set of thinking.

For players, and indeed anyone at the organisation, the biggest part of a successful well-being approach is buy-in. If you believe in what you're doing and you choose to do it, you are far more likely to be successful with it than if someone tells you to do it.

"Whether they are sporting or corporate organisations, well-being should be made opt-in; meaning that it should be the athletes' (or employees') choice as to whether or not they participate. Of course the organisation needs to sell the benefits of being involved in a well-being programme to the person and then let people choose whether they want to opt in," Johnson says. "The question you might to want to ask yourself beforehand is, why would they want to? I believe that if you can create a powerful reason why it's worthwhile, then of course people are going to be interested. Who doesn't want to learn and grow and move towards their potential as a person, particularly if you're allowed to move toward that potential in alignment with your values? One of the most underrated things sporting organisations can do is help people become more self-aware and by helping people to do so and be more confident in that self-awareness creates this amazing capacity for growth."

For coaches, often it is a change in thinking that is required. Coaches need to remember they're coaching a person not only an athlete. A big part of the problem in elite sport is short-term thinking has become chronic in many high-performance environments. Contracts based on a requirement for instant results rather than long-term, sustainable development has made many sports sick with unrealistic expectation. Much of that falls on the shoulders of the head coach.

During the global pandemic, Johnson has been delivering help to coaches around the world. One of his observations was how much self-awareness coaches lack. In order for them to consider their players or their staff as people, they need to do the same for themselves.

"How do you regulate your own emotions, how do you manage boundaries, how do you focus your attention and how do you manage stress? If you start there, then that's a great place and you can work with your team and your players and more effectively manage the organisation."

Johnson has noticed that some coaches are already further along. Those who know how to solve complex problems, think long term, build relationships and have an understanding for human motivation, consider his approach to well-being logical. Smart coaches get it, and more often than not, they are younger.

"The assistant coaches of today will be the head coaches of tomorrow," Johnson says. "So it's important to get them to think beyond the safety net. The next step is getting them conversant with well-being strategies and tools that will enable their organisations to be proactive, holistic in their approach, and ensuring their well-being staff have the capability to deliver."

Unlike coaches and players, clubs by their nature can be much harder to convince. If the simple notion that building a community of people working in elite sport who believe in the person is fundamentally a good thing isn't enough, then turning talk to investment will likely help.

"I don't see it as a cost because if I fund well-being in my organisation what I'm effectively doing is minimising time to effectiveness and building engagement with the organisation," Johnson says. "When an organisation invests in athlete well-being it increases discretionary effort, the extra effort athletes are willing to put in. In addition, having a robust well-being strategy and processes in place can be an additional piece to attract new sponsors or partners that the organisation may not have been able to attract before. Well-being can be a value-add to an organisation's package, or even a revenue stream when we run community-based programmes that we can get funding for. It's got multiple opportunities for return on investment, the most obvious one being the attraction and retention of players."

After just one conversation with Johnson it feels like I have stumbled across the holy grail of human development in sport. The concept of well-being Johnson wants to implement feels like it includes parts of all the various approaches I had learned about up until this point. The use of values ties into what AIK are doing in Sweden, the room for character development is linked to what I found out in Denmark, the realisation for coaches that they are coaching people not athletes echoes all the academy coaches I spoke to. It was so encouraging to know that this work exists and is already being implemented in professional sport.

While transition programmes for athletes leaving sport can help, this approach suffers not because of those working in the field but rather the field itself. Afterwards we can only do so much; we apply bandages to deep wounds. A well-being department built into a club's philosophy and weekly training plan allows us to deal with those injuries before they run too deep.

"This is a journey of experiences, reflection, relationships and exploration," Johnson says of a professional sports career. "As you go through that journey, you go through that sense of who am I now and who am I thinking I might want to be in the future?"

We cannot afford to encourage unidimensional thinking. There is so much more going on than what happens on the field and if we continue to foster a way of thinking that encourages players to just "stick to their football" then we are ignoring their humanness. We are going to reinforce the idea of athletes becoming machines.

Formula One is perhaps one of the most expensive pursuits, but unlike footballers, racing drivers are actually in machines. While this makes discussions about man and machine only natural, the danger of ignoring and neglecting the human remains.

Lewis Hamilton is the most successful driver in F1 history. Clearly there are other factors at play, but in 2018 on the Formula One *Beyond the Grid* podcast he said his success is partly because he isn't all about the driving. That variation stimulates his mind.

"If I spend this week just training twice a day, just sacrificing everything and not doing the things that I also like, skip them and get to the next race, physically I might be in better shape but I'm actually miserable. And if I do all the things... You should see my schedule. I'm travelling here and there, I've got these meetings, different projects that I'm working on, I get to interact and my mind is being challenged all the time so I arrive at the next race and maybe I have slightly less energy but mentally I'm buzzing and that is more powerful than having all the rest you could possibly want. I've tried it. I've been at home, done this training, turned up and just had a basic weekend. And I've been and done all these other things, and I've tried it multiple times, and it turned out much, much better."

Each sport is different, as is each character. Ultimately, Hamilton's approach does not definitively prove that racing drivers would be more successful if they didn't just stick to the track. There is obviously far more to success than just balancing focus. The superior nature of Hamilton's car and the confidence he has because of so much success for example, also plays a role. However, it does show that athletes can compete at the top level without having to solely focus on their sport. Mentally it is important, and in Hamilton's case necessary, to stimulate the brain through other activities. Furthermore, this helps the individual develop their character so that once their sporting career is over that brain stimulation stands them in good stead to both feel more comfortable about themselves and perhaps find another purpose. Perhaps, as Hugo Scheckter mentioned, many are willing or must pay the price of their humanness to succeed but with the right people and structures in place perhaps it is possible to find and nurture that humanness again.

Imagine the scenario. Bayern Munich are at the start of the season. The head coach has made it clear what kind of football he wants to play. The coaching staff have outlined their targets in terms of fitness, nutrition, and mental stability. And then the well-being manager enters.

"Okay boys, I would like to introduce you to our new well-being programme. The goal of the programme is to help you move toward your potential as a person in a way that reflects your values. By participating in this programme you will learn about yourself, relationships, life and the things that really matter to you. You don't have to participate in it but if you do we can promise that we will teach you skills that will help you feel good and function well." Johnson says. "I would like you to take some time to think about whether you'd like to be involved in this programme. If you decide you do we'll do everything we can to make sure your aspirations are made a reality. It's got nothing to do with your performance because that's to do with the coaching staff. This is about you as a person, your family and the people who are important to you and what's important in your life outside of football. There will come a day when you'll be an ex-player and we want you to have those skills so you can pass them on to your kids and to your families. So I will come back to you in a week or two and see what you think. You get to decide. It's not compulsory."

Perhaps this dream is still some years from becoming a reality. When it comes though, we will ask ourselves why it took us so long to implement - in our sports teams, businesses, for each other and our souls. If we are serious about looking after human beings, we have to care about well-being. Change is coming. Johnson is sure of it.

"I've never been more certain of anything in my life, and it's going to take a while, but that is where it's headed."

A couple of weeks later, I spoke to Paul Heptonstall, the man in charge of Australia's national rugby league (NRL) well-being and education program. Listening to him it was evident how much he loves rugby league, and how much he has done to change the culture of a sport desperately in need of aid.

Rugby league players became full time professionals in Australia in 1996, which changed the game entirely. Player salaries tripled, cars got bigger, training more serious. Suddenly, being a footie player in Australia was all you were.

Three years later, the NRL introduced their first ever national welfare and education manager, and the Wests Tigers employed their first ever welfare officer, Heptonstall. A school teacher by trade, Heptonstall had also played a bit himself in his younger years. Initially, Paul's job was focused on career planning, but for all that time spent preparing people for what Paul neatly calls "the inevitable tap on the shoulder" he realised he was spending more time helping people with their problems. "I realised there were a lot of troubled souls."

Indeed, much about the NRL at the start of the millennium was troubling. A flood of sexual assault and rape charges saw questions asked about the kind of men playing the sport, how such a toxic culture could have developed, and whether it was possible to change such monstrous and damaging incidents.

Heptonstall admits it took years before the game woke up to the idea of duty of care. Nevertheless, by 2008, a national counselling service had been in play for eight years, grant funding for education to professional players had increased, and the NRL had introduced its first youth tournament that included compulsory work and study rules in order to eligible to play.

While a great and necessary starting point, it was clear that if well-being was to take a more prominent role then learning the science was required.

Initially, well-being managers required career coaching certification and to be mental health first aiders. In 2012, funding was approved for the mandatory placement of a career coach and well-being manager at each of the 16 NRL clubs, with one usually an ex pro able to use their experience to help others and the other someone invested and qualified to help holistically. By 2018, the strength of the role had really developed. Now, players had the option to customise a well-being plan and well-being managers had to have completed the elite athlete well-being management course run by the Well-being Science Institute.

"We had to look at what makes a person feel really content, what makes them feel valued and connected? It wasn't just about careers or money. It was about community, cultural connection, spirituality, genuine relationships. We really had to dig into that side of things," Heptonstall tells me.

Faith, family and community emerged as leading sources of contentment, something impacted by an extremely diverse playing group. Australia's Indigenous population is two percent but around 10 percent of NRL players, and a third of the national team. That, combined with 45 percent of rugby league players having pacific heritage, meant work had to be done to compensate for an inevitable disconnect players were having from their community and faith.

"We're a jack of all trades but it's during those times we develop relationships. You invest yourself in more than just a clinical environment," says Heptonstall, who swapped the front line for the top job around a decade ago.

In Australia, the NRL is a small, relative young, community league that benefits from not being in the limelight the way cricket or Aussie rules is. Heptonstall uses the word malleable.

"We've struck at the right time and we've done it in a very credible way," Heptonstall says. "Some of those other sports say to us 'How did you do it?' And I think it's because we were small. I think everyone is catching up but we had the courage to jump in and do it and we were given the mandate to do it. Other sports are chasing people in the car park to meet up with players. We're walking through the front door. Their CEOs are saying, 'We've got well-being in here today, you've got to listen.' We've got our funding and our credibility."

The size, the financial support and the credible nature of the work has given the NRL the chance to do something other leagues and organisations can only talk about. They have found a way to combine winning and living in professional sport. They have embedded a philosophy.

For Heptonstall, the single most important part of this development is the introduction of an independent committee that oversees well-being in the game. This meant the introduction of well-being was not part of a deal but rather a decision made by and for the good of the game.

"We were this independent group, this Switzerland if you like that was neutral," Heptonstall says. "We didn't force things, we just tried to get it evolved."

The evolution was that along with the players' association, the clubs and the governing body (NRL), the independent committee set the standards for rugby league in Australia. If everyone is involved then it matters to everyone and with the money in a central pot those standards are accompanied by financial implications.

"We were able to do this because we convinced the game that they needed to invest in it and we were able to hold the clubs accountable with funding if they didn't do it," Heptonstall explains, adding that ranking teams by their success and investment in well-being was a key factor. "Those teams high on the well-being scale were often top of the competition ladder. Year after year, we had a couple of clubs who heavily invested in it and they were always up the top, and the clubs who didn't invest in it were down the bottom."

This is one of many sliding doors moments for the NRL. Adding a financial incentive into it may appear like missing the point of human development, but playing sport at its own game appears one shrewd way of solving the issue of not looking after the person.

After all, the idea behind making well-being necessary and something that if not done properly could lead to funding being withheld was that teams would see the value in looking after people. In turn, this would provide more stability, a better club and a greater chance of success. Had the teams who had invested heavily in it not ended up winning, this concept might never have taken root. Instead, the NRL now offers one of the most holistic approaches in modern, professional sport.

In 2012, every one of the 16 NRL clubs had a rule in place that the members of their U20 team had to work or study at least three days a week in order to be eligible to play. The majority of these players are now in the professional game, but 20 percent of them are also at university and between 15 to 20 percent of them have learned trades. In doing so, the NRL has created an active and sustainable pathway for both the person and the player. They have created opportunities, and clubs who nurture this pathway - one where the four pillars of career development, mental health, well-being and social responsibility begin - can also receive financial incentive.

It doesn't stop there either. At the start of 2020, Heptonstall and his team introduced new standards for the pro game. The top 30 players are on a salary cap but must still have one full day and another half day a week invested in work or study. The six development players in the squad must have two days off a week (one full day and two half days) and anyone in the squad who is 20 or younger must complete one day of work or study a week.

Of course, there is room for flexibility and while players get their training schedules weeks in advance sometimes it is not always possible to fulfil the standards. "We have sold the fact that a better player means a better game," Heptonstall says.

'Clubs know they must invest a certain amount into well-being for their 36 players. Heptonstall delivers the framework, and the well-being managers and their respective clubs decide how best to put it into action.

Between 2014 and 2018, the NRL has won national awards for career development, alcohol management strategy, pride in diversity and spiritual leadership. And yet, despite awards and ever expanding framework, the image that haunted the NRL at the start of the millennium remains.

As stated in *news.com.au*, the Australian media has reported on 66 separate allegations of rugby league players behaving poorly, at times unacceptably since the beginning of 2015. In 2019, the league's CEO Todd Greenberg called that year's preseason a "complete train wreck" after an alleged assault, a sex tape scandal and an entire team were banned for alleged bad behaviour. More incidents followed in 2020. It is a reminder that despite the advanced nature of the NRL's approach to well-being and support, there is still a lot of work to do.

Inevitably, the increasing money in the game has made it harder and harder to set minimum times aside for well-being work. Well-being managers are not only trying to do their job every day but also regularly have to justify why their job matters. This is surprising given the raft of scandals the league has faced in recent years, as is the fact that some coaches are questioning the need for well-being when many of them are where they are because of support. "We tell them they have a duty of care. Don't be a hypocrite," Heptonstall says.

It seems obvious that perhaps now more than ever this work is important, and it is also work that takes a toll. There is a psychologist who checks in on the well-being managers to make sure they are looked after, but when I spoke to Heptonstall in early 2021 one of his staff had just had a breakdown.

"My fear is if we took our foot off the gas a little bit, clubs would come back a little bit. It's a constant process. You've got to be there all the time and reminding people of the importance," Heptonstall says. The pandemic certainly didn't help but despite losing 25 percent of his central budget, Heptonstall made sure most of the well-being managers were kept at clubs.

"The thing I'm most proud of is that we have a well-being community and it's not just about you winning, it's about us as a game," Heptonstall says. "For me, it's as much about the game as it is the person because I want my kids to play rugby league in a good environment, so I want the environment to be supportive and better. There was always this motive that you just want the game to be better. When mums and dads have less influence on their kids, you want the game to be able to deliver."

On the field, the NRL has delivered much excitement over the years but off it issues have remained. The introduction of this well-being approach hasn't turned rugby league in Australia into a sport free of issues, nor could it ever do so alone but Heptonstall and his team have created a framework backed by science, delivered by qualified professionals and with financial accountability that is doing its best to help turn the tide. Not many sports can say the same when it comes to looking after the person.

7

Switzerland

In football, there is one job where human development tends to be an afterthought. A job where time is limited, expectations are huge and your performance can create enormous social waves. International management is a world where perhaps results matter the most, but as with any team, failure to consider the individual will make success less likely.

I was set to spend some time with Switzerland's women's national team and their Danish head coach Nils Nielsen in April 2020, but then the pandemic began to intensify in Europe and the chance was gone. Just shy of a year later, Nielsen and I did have the chance to talk and while video calls can never replace the real thing, hearing how he approaches human development on the international stage was fascinating.

"If you always tell someone what to do, 2+2 will be 3. If you teach them, 2+2 is 4, but if you involve them and use their strengths and they really learn about themselves and their teammates, 2+2 is 5," Nielsen tells me, referring to the phrase that is often wrongly attributed to Benjamin Franklin. The proverb actually comes from Xunzi, one of the great Confucian philosophers in ancient China. What was originally written as "I hear I forget, I see I remember, I do I understand", Franklin attributed as "Tell me and I forget, teach me and I may remember, involve me and I learn."

With an earring and a short haircut, Nielsen looks like a Danish rockstar. His methods are nowhere near as loud though. He believes in the long game, and while sometimes he reverts to the teaching approach in order to win because winning brings confidence, Nielsen has largely stuck to what he believes in and that is looking after the person.

Having coached youth football in Denmark, Nielsen then embarked on a successful career in women's football. First he took Denmark's national team to the 2017 European Championship final, then after leading China's U20s to the 2018 U20 World Cup only a last-minute own goal denied them a spot in the knockouts. Since September 2018, he has been in charge of the Swiss team. In each country his greatest challenge has been recognising where people of other cultures are coming from, something he believes is pivotal to any attempt at human development.

In Denmark, Nielsen was at home. He knew the school system and life in the country. Connecting with the team wasn't a problem, but it was the overly critical nature of the Danish team that made human development hard to redesign.

"It was no problem getting them to talk, sometimes the problem was getting them to stop talking," Nielsen says. "The first game I had with them, we were watching a video afterwards as part of our evaluation. We had just played a good game, but after one and a half hours of talking I had to stop them. They were so hard on themselves about little details that didn't really matter and it was the first meeting, they didn't even know me."

In China, Nielsen experienced quite the opposite. The Dane found there was a wall of respect that was put up which made emotional connection difficult, especially when combined with the language barrier. Formal meetings didn't help and so walks to the training pitch became the one place where Nielsen and his staff could attempt to break down some barriers: "We needed them to understand we were there for them."

In Switzerland, Nielsen naturally needed a different approach. After all, with every new country comes a new culture and methodology. When he first arrived with his current team, he had to help a group of women come out of their shell.

"We are trying to find symbols because the culture here is completely different. The women have been suppressed in a way you cannot understand if you haven't been there," Nielsen says.

Half of his staff are women but in team meetings if those women are speaking, the others do not pay attention. Nielsen notes that if he says the same thing five minutes later, the response is often: "What a great idea."

It was only 50 years ago that Swiss women got the right to vote. Indeed, one of Switzerland's most influential feminist activists, Zita Küng, told Germany's international broadcaster DW in 2021 that when women eventually won the right to vote they needed a majority of Swiss men to accept a woman's right to vote. Given that the right to vote is just one part of gender equality, Swiss women, like most women in the world, are still fighting for that fairness.

"They have been used to not being heard," Nielsen says. "School is not based on dialogue, it's based on learning by repeating. That doesn't encourage you to speak your mind."

In Nielsen's first training session he asked the team how they usually defended the box. What happened next was not something he was ready for, but was an example of how much an engrained culture affects understanding in how to speak to people, let alone how to coach a team.

"I had to ask five times before anyone answered," Nielsen says. "Then I realised, I need to change something here. It was always about not talking in the group but talking away from the group. We had to change talking before we changed anything else."

Interestingly, it was Nielsen's sport psychologist who sparked a pivotal idea. Having worked with the Swiss team before Nielsen's arrival, Dr Nina Jokuschies was able to help him understand Swiss culture (even though she is not Swiss). Most importantly, she helped the players realise Nielsen was there to help them and listen, not - as they expected - to shout at them.

And so Jokuschies came up with the smart idea to discuss identity without having to use themselves. By using animals, the Swiss team began to understand themselves and how a team works more. This, by all accounts, was no laughing matter either. They took it seriously.

"When they all had an animal then we could pair them up in groups and ask: 'How do we make an environment where all the animals feel good? What do we need?' We were talking about rivers and mountains and drawing it all out," Nielsen explains. "They began to understand, 'Okay, I'm a lion and I have to play with a zebra. I have to not hunt them'. We ended up talking about the way we were talking to each other. We tried to build a team with all these different characters, and make them understand that we cannot make a team with only lions, especially because some of them even went so far as to say they felt like male lions, a little lazy. They understood we're all different and we all need to be here and good."

Nielsen's experiences in other countries with other cultures will have aided his own understanding, but he knew he couldn't just tell the Swiss women to be like the Danish women.

"They feel safe being Swiss so you have to take little steps with them and say: 'Whatever we want to be we can be in our team.' The way they want to be as a team and how they act with one another, I didn't do that, they did."

This approach is the more demanding and time-consuming road to human development but - like any decision - to make this a priority bumps are to be expected. Other than one or two experienced players, the team often suffered from insecurity.

Again this was because they were not used to taking responsibility and so Nielsen and his team had to approach developing the team through the person. He wanted his team to come out of their shell and so quite literally asked them to do so.

"We used the oyster because an oyster with a little sand grain in it creates a pearl, but if you don't open the oyster and let people see it then it might as well not be there."

Nielsen's great turn of phrase is a constant throughout our conversation, and it must add another layer of confidence to his players if he speaks to them in a similar fashion.

In a game against a good opponent, Nielsen brought a player back from injury and played her in a new position. She was completely lost and stressed. Nielsen, who normally asks the team why rather than telling them to react differently, was frustrated because not one player in the team helped her. He asked why the team had left their teammate to suffer and not jumped in to help. He asked one of his strikers to lift up her hair and he told the team, 'She hasn't got an eye there, she can't see the game behind her.' The team laughed, and that was when Nielsen realised the striker actually had a tattoo of an eagle with a huge eye in that exact spot. "It was really funny but they got the point. Even a really experienced player needs help on the pitch and if no one is helping then we play one against 11 eleven times."

Here Nielsen's attempts to help the team on the field were made possible by his decision to review both the individual's and the collective's identity. Without this, the oyster never opens. Help and support off the field will always lead to better performance on it, and his coaching career is full of examples where he has put the person before the player.

Six months ago he got an email from a player he used to coach who, after injury troubles and a personal crisis, gave up playing and is now a physiotherapist for handicapped children and so happy. In the email she told Nielsen how much it had meant to her to be in that team and that Nielsen had asked about her problems with her dad but never let it influence his decisions on the field (what she was used to). She was grateful she had been allowed to be upset, talk and get some space.

"That is the reason why you have to have the individual in focus because not everyone becomes Pernille Harder. They still have to have a life after the game and they can learn so much from a professional environment if you encourage and don't hit them over the head every time they don't fit into boxes. They need to learn how to be themselves and what makes them happy."

Another girl he coached needed six months off to finish her education, and once she was done Nielsen welcomed her back into the national team.

"If you don't do these things and let them be in the moment but instead try and pull them in all different directions you pull them apart instead of putting them together. Everything has its time. Sometimes it's football, sometimes it is something else."

Another situation arose when one of the oldest players in his Denmark squad was unsure whether to continue or not because she was without a club. Her training performances with the national team weren't great and so Nielsen, thanks to a good relationship, approached her to talk. It turns out both she and her flatmate were unsure of their futures in the game and were struggling to put food on the table. Nielsen gave her the time to go away and sort out her life, reassuring her that her spot in the team was safe. When she returned, both she and her flatmate had contracts, she was in a better spot mentally and was then the best player on the pitch.

"Even the most experienced player in the team can have situations that have a lot more to do with something else than the game and if you don't allow them to deal with that and you play them not only do they play badly but you make it worse. Instead of saying, 'Hey, you're just as important as always for me but you're not going to play because the state of mind you have right now is keeping you from performing.'"

The point Nielsen is making is not a new one, but it is refreshing to see a head coach give the person time to deal with whatever they need to so that the player can return to their best performance. It seems logical, but given how often sport reduces itself and its athletes to results this consideration remains rare.

Pivotally, Nielsen does not believe he was able to make the decisions he did because he was working in the women's game. He believes the approach is the same, it's just the starting point that is different.

"If you are talking to a 17-year-old boy with ten million in the bank then you talk to them a different way than a 17-year-old schoolgirl because their world is different, but they have to learn the same things about being in a group and handling themselves. It's exactly the same. You just have to talk to them in a different way," Nielsen tells me, before adding: "The expectations are exactly the same for the girls, it's just different people who have those expectations."

To highlight this, Nielsen recalls yet another story from his youth coaching days at perhaps Denmark's most famous club, Brøndby. The Dane told one of the young boys to go home because he wasn't doing his homework. The talented 15-year-old thought he was somewhere he was not. His perception did not reflect his reality, but he understood, went away to study, came back into the team and ten years later he was playing in the Premier League.

"These people who you're a little bit tough on but hold a mirror up to and say: 'Listen, you want to be stupid or something you're not then that's fine but you're not in the team.' Those people remember," Nielsen says before adding that that player still sends him cards and messages, asking how Nielsen's team is doing.

"We taught them how to focus on the things that are happening right now instead of dreaming of something that might happen," Nielsen says. "That makes me sure this is the best way to develop human beings and players, to help them be the best version they can be in any situation. And if they're acting like jerks then you need to address it, even if it has nothing to do with football."

Nielsen believes people are the best version of themselves when they feel good and they understand what they are doing and why they are where they are, on the field and in life.

"Why am I spending so much time on this? They can say, 'Because I love football', but how come you are afraid? You cannot be afraid of something you love."

Nielsen's approach to human development is built off consideration for the language he uses, the importance of autonomy, and recognition that sometimes football should not be the main focus. He cares about tactics, but knows that if he doesn't consider the person and the culture within which those people operate then it doesn't matter whether he plays 4-4-2 or 3-4-3.

"Football is emotions, it's not tactics," the Dane tells me. "Any good team with the right tactic, if they're not right in the head they're going to lose... Successful tactics reflect the team's state of mind. If you want to win something, culture and identity are more important. Clubs who were good once and then had a slump are searching for their identity. They keep changing coaches but they never really say: 'We want to be this club.' They just keep trying to find a coach and buy a player that can win the championship. It is like peeing your pants on a windy day. You might win if you invest a lot of money but it becomes really cold when the wind comes because you don't have the culture. And so over time you won't win, you'll just have wasted a lot of money."

To follow Nielsen's amusing analogy, it seems that far too many football clubs are quite happy to pee their pants on a windy day. The decision to change culture, language, establish an identity and make sure everyone at the club buys into it is to consciously decide to opt for an approach that contains a lot of intangibles. It also takes the right people.

Nielsen appears to be one of those. The Dane is convinced that this is the right way to do it and the number of times he mentioned players who were grateful to have been a part of his teams is further proof that this approach matters.

"You need to help people find their way because it reflects in the game. I'm not doing it because I'm a better person than anyone else. I'm just a normal person. I'm doing it because I want to win and I know if I have the best version of everybody then we have a better chance to win."

In a paper in the *AGON International Journal of Sport Sciences*, Antonio Alvarez Zamora maintains that the high-performance athlete should not be seen only as an athlete but also as a person with psychosocial, emotional and academic/vocational development.

Quoted in *The Athletic* in November 2020, legendary coach Arsene Wenger was less scientific but equally poignant about the need to remember the person: "I thought I always approached a player as a global human being. Everything interferes. Everything is connected. If you want to know people you have to meet people, ask questions... Or you just treat him like a machine. He comes in and he has to produce."

Perhaps a lot of that machine-like treatment is done unwittingly, simply as a result of many sports reaching supercharged levels of professionalism that leave little room for humanness. Perhaps it has been done this way for so long now that to do it differently would be too much of a shock for all involved, coaches and players. Either way, a return to person first, player second is a must. Otherwise we risk sport becoming a sterilised form of entertainment totally disconnected from the real world.

Some might say some sports have already long crossed those borders, but there are those working hard to turn the tide. Nielsen is one of those, and he is conscious, perhaps even hopeful, that his work may well lead to change.

"It's like a stone in the water," Nielsen says. "If you can influence something it might spread to something else. You don't know where the wave is going but if you can help them you can also perhaps over time help the whole culture, not you personally, but what you started. That is the what we are trying to do with Swiss football. I'm ambitious, I want to win as well but the reason, as I said earlier, is that I know we get better results with people who feel good and are the best versions of themselves."

And Nielsen himself? He feels he is the best version of himself, and therefore able to do what he does, largely because of his wife. As a former professional ballet dancer, she can relate to his frustrations and helps Nielsen with his self-admitted selfishness. "She knows more about the Swiss players in the world than anyone else," quips the Dane.

Nielsen tells me she also understands why he cares because she wishes when she was a dancer someone had cared more about her than just her jumps and pirouettes. A poignant reminder that too much of the sporting world has spent too long not considering the person.

Nora Häuptle is intrigued by people. The former international player turned coach quips that perhaps the curiosity that makes her not so Swiss is why she gets on so well with Nielsen. Almost exactly a year after I spoke to the Dane, Häuptle talks to me from her apartment in Switzerland. It's been two weeks since she was sacked as head coach of Bundesliga side SC Sand. In a league with an enormous disparity between the teams at the top and the bottom of the table, Sand had given themselves a chance of survival, which for a club that always knew relegation was a possibility was encouraging. With five games to go though, the club were not convinced that chance was big enough and Häuptle was relieved of her duties.

Four days later, Sand won 6-1 and would not lose another

game in the run-in, picking up 11 points from their final five games. From a purely sporting perspective, this is vindication for the board's decision. Sand secured another year in Germany's top flight, which is a huge boost for a club with modest facilities and that struggles to retain players. However, to suggest that Häuptle's absence was the reason for Sand's upturn in fortune would be to fall into the trap of the head coach narrative. It is at this point I remember what Daniel Niedzkowski told me in *Mensch*:

'If there's no success, then everyone expects the conversation about the head coach to arise,' Niedzkowski says. 'That means others are out of the firing line because players know the first thing that will happen will be the head coach will be dismissed. When a new coach comes, players know they have to give it 100 per cent again because nobody is established anymore and everyone has a new chance, and that's why, at the start, there's an increase in performance. Those who have played before have to prove themselves again, and the players who were further down the pecking order now have a new chance. Without the head coach having done anything, the conditions are already more in his favour than before. But if the club says the current coach is staying whatever happens, then everyone else can't hope the problem will be solved for them. They have to re-engage themselves with a new situation."

The situation of each club is different but to believe that Sand avoided relegation because Häuptle was no longer there is wrong, especially considering the details. Just the day before she was released, Häuptle told me she had spoken to the team about accountability.

"I had a big speech on Monday, it was interesting to the team," Häuptle said on a video call. "Sometimes I saw them just lean on me and think everything was going to be all right because the coach is here and she'll fix it, you know. On Monday I told them: 'Listen, I have the feeling that you think I'm going to fix it for you, but I'm not going on to the pitch. You need to take responsibility. You need to take initiative.' The words hung in the air for a bit, it was quite a long speech. I thought this is going to be a hard talk, but I need to do it now, and I think this was quite good and I felt that I touched them. And then we had an excellent session Tuesday morning. And then I went into the office as the president came in and that was that. They told: 'I'm sorry, we've decided to move on.'"

For the club, the decision to sack Häuptle was their attempt at accountability, one that almost always works in favour of the organisation either way because it is a clear piece of evidence supporting action during a struggle. What it doesn't do is prove that was the issue that needed solving, as Niedzkowski rightly reminds us.

What is more concerning is that Häuptle believed she had been given the chance to build something beyond a team that won games. She arrived believing her values were matched by the club, encouraged by a team that wanted to do things differently. And yet the moment pressure increases, especially somewhere with limited financial resources, the importance of values can shift.

"I always say in the beginning, I start with values, because you can never trade your values," Häuptle tells me. "When you trade them, then there's nothing and you see clubs that trade their values, it's the beginning of the end. And I didn't understand this part of that because it was a place where it was special, because people are passionate," Häuptle explains about a club that is still somewhat amateur to a certain extent. "And now they trade their own values... But it shows me it's a bit of an end of an era, and then maybe it is better I'm not there."

Häuptle acknowledges that Sand lost a lot of games under her as coach, that she needed to refine patterns and that at the beginning perhaps she tried to change too much of the things that weren't working. However, she put a developmental approach into place and was working towards something that leads to wins later but requires patience and understanding: "You always know where to go when you have development goals. You can lose the next week but you know where to go back to. You always have your values, the foundation, but then you always know what to work on next. And this gives you a dynamic in the process which never ends."

One of the ways in which Häuptle did this was to speak to her players about who they were as people. She gave them a book by John Strelecky called *The Big Five For Life*, which sparked a conversation about legacy and the five things they would want to see in the "museum of their life" at the end. Häuptle posed the question 'What is it to have a good life?' and every week a player presented their "Big Five" in the form of a presentation or a video.

"They did crazy things and this was so interesting because first it was funny, because they are so creative. If you give them a bit of feeling, they do things you can never imagine. And you learn a lot about the people because then I just see these dreams or visions and how really important they are for them. You see another picture, another surface, another variation of the human in front of you and which you never sometimes discover when it's just chatter based on play. And so these Big Fives were always important and there was a curiosity about the next presentation. This was something we enjoyed a lot."

This exploration will have done more for those players than extra training sessions ever could. It's probably also the reason why when Häuptle was fired, she received written letters from her players. Häuptle also received support from other coaches in Switzerland, and the show of solidarity helped remind her of the value of her work.

That is something Häuptle never had when she was playing. Like many who played in the early 2000s or earlier, conversations about holistic development were few and far between, particularly in women's football. Back then, you either reflected or you didn't. There were very few people in sport checking in with you beyond performance.

"I learned a lot in the last year," Häuptle tells me. "Because when you play you don't reflect on those things too much, I didn't, so as a coach I thought more and learned that it's very interesting. To know more about the people, because when you understand motives, desires, fears, all those things that happen in every human, then you understand much more about why a player cannot perform in the moment... I was curious and I always want to develop or learn. And so when you realise you are not good at relationships, for example, then you need to ask yourself about your balance. I think it all starts with you. Why do you have fear, and about what? How is your family structure? All those things, I think are so interesting to know, to understand you better. You need to work on yourself first, I think."

While aware of what a privilege it is to grow up in Switzerland, calling the place an island of sorts, Häuptle's ability to create and decide what to do early on helped her as both a person and a coach. Aided by open-minded parents who didn't know anything about football and just let her do it, Häuptle felt she was able to find balance in life more easily.

"In days like this, I'm very happy that I learned this part quite early in my coaching career, because then it's not taking your whole foundation away when you get fired like this, because you have other values you count on, you have other things you define yourself through. And then when something is breaking, it's not that your whole world is breaking down. That's my approach to living a good life. I stay curious and I realise there's so many things to discover, and I think that's a bit my show on my way to see life. And then it's not all about football. This is a bit the sense just to live a good life. This is just the journey itself. We are always looking for the it, but it's the journey, you know, this experience which I made and to get better and to pick five."

Häuptle isn't sure of all the five in her life but knows they will change over time, although family and her partner will likely always remain. Perhaps the curiosity and enjoyment she gets from renovating bathtubs won't (she has one in development on the balcony when we talk) but that doesn't matter. Häuptle is enjoying it for now and that's also enough.

For Sand, Häuptle was not enough, which begs the question what is? If sport is only about winning then we are headed in a dangerous direction. Clearly in competition the desire and determination to win is necessary and an enjoyable reason why so many watch and play sport, but to make it the sole focus, particularly to the detriment of values and beliefs cannot be the answer from sport or life.

Ultimately it is less about whether Sand were right or wrong to sack Häuptle and more what does Sand want to represent as a football club? Every club wants to win but what is it about you that makes you worth supporting, coaching, or playing for? Great players, excellent facilities, wonderful fans - all important motivations but again, many clubs can offer the same. What is it that truly sets you apart?

Häuptle is set apart by her curiosity and her desire to integrate life into coaching. When she was fired, words from Hope Powell, a coaching mentor and friend, helped. Powell told her not to be surprised by the emotions that would change in her. She was angry, sad and then calm. Throughout it all though, she never lost sight of who she was and that is someone who cares about the person.

8

Cost

After listening to and speaking with so many people doing work to help human beings, I began to wonder what happens if we don't look after the person? What happens if the sheer nature of an environment is so confined to ruthlessly pursuing victory that anything not directly connected to that is deemed unnecessary?

In early 2021, Blackburn Rovers' Head of Athletic Performance, Chris Rush, quit working in football after he realised it was costing him too much. After 15 years in the sport, Rush walked away because the sacrifice to his family was too great.

Writing on LinkedIn, Rush said: "My decision is purely based on wanting to prioritise family life over my professional life. The life of a support staff member in football requires 60+ hour work weeks, 11 months a year, weekends away from the family, and missed life events."

This is likely no surprise for those who work in football, or high-performance pressurised environments, but the reality remains a damning assessment. Everyone working at an organisation is a person and for it to narrow its field of assessment to just performance is not only inhuman, but also likely to result in a worse performance outcome.

So often I had seen online courses about how to make yourself mentally tougher. They undoubtedly contained some valid lessons but whenever I read "be feared rather than liked" and "don't celebrate achievements because you always want more" all I could see was the dehumanisation of the athlete. The message is as clear as ever. If you want to be in this space and excel you have to sacrifice that human part of you.

The same is asked of coaches. Humanness in exchange for the chance to work in a high-performance world is a price football and sport generally does not have to pay. Sadly though, it is one that it keeps paying, and willingly so. In early 2021 when I spoke to Rush he confirmed as much when I asked him whether he felt he had to give up a humanness to work in football.

"It sounds terrible to say, but yeah," Rush says over a video call in March 2021. "For the last four years at Blackburn I managed the department, not just an individual fitness coach, and there were times I can remember coming away from days thinking my actions with a staff member didn't represent me, but that's the pressure on you to do the job and you can pass it on. It's a very macho environment, not as much as 15 years ago, but

I still think it's definitely not a normal working place. There's stuff going on all the time, conversations, arguments, they can get taken on and passed down the food chain. I read a lot of books about different things, including Buddhism, and it's really difficult to apply, let's say that calmness, to the environment without feeling the perception of 'you're too laid back'."

Granted this is one club and one scenario but many other coaches have made similar comments. The idea of mindfulness is great but just make sure it doesn't stop you working 12-hour days. It is telling that Rush was at his most relaxed once he had informed the club of his decision to leave. That move changed how he acted and his observations of the environment around him.

"You start to see things. You lose a game and you come in. I've just had breakfast with the kids, been laughing and joking and dancing around the house, I arrive in a great mood and go into the indoor pitch with 50 people inside and no one is speaking to anybody. You feel you cannot be happy, openly happy, because the perception would be you're happy because we've lost, you're not serious enough. That's a big reason why it's different to other businesses, because of that intense analysis of performance every four to five days."

As Rush rightly points out, there is a great deal of scientific evidence and real-life examples that the leading high-performance environments consider behavioural psychology. That is not to say the club didn't try to do more in human development. Performance coaches came in, psychological profiles were created and there was an opportunity for everyone to improve their understanding of personalities, responses and relationship management. For something to take root though, not only do you need a bit of luck but you also need it to be a part of regular, everyday life at the club.

"Some people in that environment don't really like that, don't like the depth," Rush says. "They believe, 'We just need to get better players, we just need to coach better. We're doing all this stuff over here and it's just confusing everybody.' It's that short term versus long term reality. Going down that road in the short term will lead to some pushback and confusion as people understand the reasons for it. If you win ten games in a row whilst doing that it probably stays forever. If you lose a lot of games it's probably out the door really quickly."

The root of the problem is that the basis for this approach is not a genuine belief in the idea. Tacking on human development as if it were another session is unlikely to bring the kind of change the idea is designed for, let alone increase performance. Organisations need to be led by people who not only believe in human development but also put that belief into action. Without it, the non-performance part of life will be neglected. People will only ever be viewed through the numerical value of their contribution.

"When I finally decided to say I was going to finish in football, the manager and the CEO were completely shocked because they didn't think I would be in that place," Rush says, tellingly. Clubs are willing to push people beyond their professional limits in pursuit of achieving performance goals but are not willing to check what that might cost.

Rush recognised that much time away from his family was not a price he wanted to pay any more. After a couple of years of considering the idea, life in lockdown during the global pandemic was the deciding moment for Rush.

"It's okay thinking you want more time with the family and weekends off but you might get bored after two or three weekends. All my adult life all I've ever done is working in football. There was still a part of me that was still unsure, was it grass is greener sort of mentality? But then lockdown happened and I was in my house with my family for months on end and if anything's going to tell you where you sit on it... Once we came out of that period and it was time to go back I wasn't really ready to go back. I had enjoyed that time with them so much. Initially when we went back, from my role on the fitness side, there was a lot of work to be done so you chuck yourself back in to it. It was great for the first few weeks but then I got to a point, the games started and I just thought this isn't catching me again. I've seen the other side of things and I realised that's actually what I want, a bit more normality in life."

For Rush, that normality was being with his family. "My kids are becoming proper little human beings and you increasingly feel like you're missing things with them just because of the nature of the job."

However much an expectation it may be in high-performance environments, it is shocking that this sacrifice is never a question for those handing out the opportunities. It's almost always: 'This is the job, this is high-performance, this is football.' So often we hear about the high-performance environments of the world but so rarely do we hear about the cost of being in those spaces.

"The reality is, the expectation is if you work in football then it is 60, 70 work weeks," Rush says. "It doesn't have to be but why it is that way is because there's almost a feeling that you're lucky to work in football, especially if you're not a player or an ex-player. If you've got that opportunity then the feeling is you should be working every hour god sends. On the flipside, I understand the nature of any high-performance environment. If you want to succeed and push, internally you can apply your own pressure to work this 60, 70 hour work week because there's never enough hours in the day to do everything. There's always another research paper to read, something else to do. The pressure can be both external in terms of expectations and internal because of the demand you put on yourself as well."

Rush admits his restless nature is a big driving force in creating internal pressure that is common in high-performance environments. People are motivated to be in that space and then want to do all the work they can and more. Much like the athlete, they feel they must use every minute possible to improve.

But the influence of the external environment on the individual, particularly over time, is not to be underestimated. High-performance spaces are often relentless, but it is those that are holistic that tend to be the most effective. Just focussing on victory is a narrow perspective, and if the entire atmosphere at a club is focussed on one goal then over time the external influence starts to dictate how people feel they must behave and therefore plays a role in the development of internal pressure.

"Externally, I do think the culture when you're working with a football club is very team result centred," Rush tells me. "Everything is sacrificed for the team winning and we've all got to be willing to make that sacrifice, which especially when people have tough times in their lives for whatever reason is pretty difficult."

Furthermore, that often leads organisations to opt for younger people who might perhaps have fewer external factors in their lives and are willing to sacrifice more because of the opportunity. This is not a unique issue to sport nor does it mean that younger candidates are not qualified or right for the job, but it does mean that more experienced professionals are often forced to sacrifice equilibrium for the job.

Ultimately the question is, whose job is it to make these decisions? As Steve Johnson rightly pointed out in chapter six, if it comes from the top then true philosophical change is far more likely. That doesn't have to be the CEO, as the case of Stuart Webber at Norwich City shows, but often if the most senior person is willing to make those decisions then the entire philosophy of a place can change. Getting there though, is the hard part.

"I've worked with some brilliant people who are very much of the mindset of trying to do these things but they may just be in the wrong position in the club without the level of influence, which then means it's very difficult to implement," Rush rightly points out.

"Dominant philosophy within a club plays a big role. You see amazing mission statements and values at these huge businesses and if they're held true to then I'm sure it's an amazing place to work. Football clubs are community-based. In an hour's circumference of where I live there might be 15 professional football teams, all with their own individual communities. That offers opportunities. I would almost say because football teams are so embedded in their communities they should be non-profit organisations because they are a source of happiness for the community. If you bring that into the philosophy of the club... Now, fans want to win games but I think there is more to football than just that, why people go to games and support a team. There should definitely be more to it than that for people who want to work in it as well. That is nowhere near the mindset at the moment."

This is partly, as Rush explains, because regardless of the position you have people at clubs who are employed to do a technical job. The CEO, for example, considers the financial prudence of the club, how the club's being marketed, but why are they not considering aspects of a leadership model based on people, behaviours and values?

The focus on the technical aspect is important but to solely do so is a steps towards further separation of departments rather than synergising. Clearly, one person cannot do everything and delegating to expertise is important but there needs to be synergy between everyone. Rush believes that ultimately the people who have merged technical with personal have done so by stepping away from the purely technical demands of the job.

"With more and more experience you realise improving is less about increasing your technical ability and knowledge and more about the soft skills, the behavioural, relationships, creating buy-in, adaptability. It's not the super-technical person that stands out," Rush says.

Imagine a CEO who is not just focussed on selling tickets or bringing in the right players, but rather one who is capable of delegating such work to experts who fit the values he wants the club to transmit so that he can focus on creating and maintaining an environment that considers the human.

"Say someone buys Blackburn and says, we're not going to live and die by what division we're in, how many games we win and lose. Of course, we're going to build systems to ensure we win games but this is the actual principal behind the football club, say provide pride to the community. If that becomes your mission for the football club then a lot of the stuff we're talking about also is much easier to implement. Then you look to hire a manager who embodies those things rather than the one with the best win percentage and you give them time. In fact, as long as I see him holding true to those values and the team is performing, well he's got a job for a long time. That's the fundamental shift you need to see for this to become a reality."

Football remains a long way from that moment though, with many modern clubs being treated as a way to market a product or a country, generate multiple income streams or join an elite group of people.

On this point Rush references author Simon Sinek's idea of the circle of safety. Leaders draw a circle around a group of people to bond them together in the face of external pressure and threats. That requires risk but leads to innovation because the ability to fail without fear of losing your job leads to more creativity. The key factors are who is in the circle and how big is it? If everyone inside shares the same values and everyone is included then an organisation is more likely to change and progress collectively rather than in fits and starts. Too often though, only a select few are in the group and the values they want to protect are in their interest rather than the organisations. A small group of people who just want to make sure they eat rather than feed everyone is a guaranteed way to avoid human development.

"In a football club, your circle of security can be quite small," Rush explains from his experience. "From a support staff level outside of coaches, managers and players, that could even be financial, emotional. You've got managers or coaches or players who are highly pressured from the external world and passing that on to you and you feel emotionally challenged and not secure. For me, everybody is looked after and everyone is in the circle of security, where people feel confident, comfortable and motivated."

I wonder whether Rush might have felt differently had the kind of structure Steve and Paul told me about been in place. He believes it would have helped, but it wouldn't have stopped him still being asked to commit to the kind of hours that ultimately made him miss family events. For a club though, Rush was all in on the idea.

"That approach sounds great from an emotional, health performance perspective. Even with the performance hat on, everyone still knows a happy, comfortable, confident staff member or footballer is always going to perform better than someone who feels under pressure or unloved," Rush says.

In one of the last training sessions Rush was a part of, he saw this truth in action. "On a Friday, the team does tactical shape work. The starting eleven has been named and we're going through the last little bits, patterns of play. The team that hasn't been picked to start the next day are always miles better than the team that has been picked to start. The manager asked one of the players why the team he hasn't picked always looks like Brazil? The answer was because we've got freedom to play, we don't have to think about any tactical information. We're not thinking about what tomorrow is going to bring and the pressure. We can just play football, and the other team is the opposite."

Towards the end of his time in football, Rush was able to just work, free of pressure. Rush knew football wasn't going to wait for him. After so many years in the same job, change was bringing him fulfilment. When we spoke he was learning and doing work on the house he and his partner had just bought. When talking about his family and this new life Rush smiled more than he had at any other point of the call.

Variety may well be part of the reason Rush decided to leave football, but for those still into sport it's also the key to a more well-balanced life and ultimately better performance.

"There's nothing healthy about being a professional athlete because you feel like you should dedicate every minute of every day to being the best you can at that and that isn't healthy," Rush says. "I can only speak to myself and actually my ultimate goal working in football was to be the best fitness coach I could be, whatever that looked like. I think I got better as a fitness coach the more time I spent reading books that were linked to personal development, books that opened me up to different things in the world and not just a funnel of technicality and executing. My performance has been better when I've been in that place, over and above 'what were the body fats today?'"

Tom Dent feels the same. The 30-year-old Englishman is head coach of first division (second tier) side Stjørdals-Blink and knows his success is determined by much more than the X's and O's. He makes it clear to me how proud he is of this when we speak in the spring of 2021 because, despite his age, this young man also paid a price for a life in football.

Two years ago, a year before the pandemic, Dent spent his first Christmas away from the family. His defensive mechanism kicked in. If he was too busy he wouldn't have time to miss home. So he did courses, analysed games, read books. It was mentally exhausting, and although he learned more about himself and unwittingly prepared himself for the pandemic it was a turning point in his life. Dent knew for too long football had been his life.

"When I first moved to Norway people always asked me did you find the transition hard? The answer I gave was no because the only thing I was thinking about when I was 21 was 'I'm going to work in football full time.' That was it, and because I was on my own, it [football] consumed my thoughts," Dent says.

"People talk about what they identify themselves as and I totally get it. For that part of my life, I was a coach. If I didn't have coaching, who was I? If I had a football conversation I was happy but if I had to talk about where I went on holiday last year then it wasn't that easy."

When Dent got home from football he was immediately thinking about how to get more football out of the rest of the day. "I felt I had to use the time. If I was working from 9-6, when I got home I felt I had to read a book or an article or find a game. I think my episode was a consequence of years of doing that and not adapting to life."

Up until that point, Dent's life had been family and football, and in his pursuit of the latter he found himself moving away from the former. But if Dent had never left, his coaching career would have ended. He would hit what he likes to call the glass ceiling.

"If you make it past the glass ceiling - working in a first team - then I think you can survive in the game in your older years. If you don't make it past or decide not to push past, then it's difficult."

For Dent, the conversation about coaches is the same one being had about youth players. "Some make it to the first team and once they make it there they tend to stay. If they don't and they get released they have to go the long way round, which can still be at a senior team but at a much lower level and they will likely have to do something on the side."

The ambition to coach in a first team can be dangerous. Dent himself found as much when he was coaching in England.

"Young coaches get too impatient in England and I can say that from experience because I worked with a senior men's team at 24 for the same reasons. But I learned very quickly that I wasn't ready for it. It's not about the football. There are many coaches who can be ready to do it from the football side. What many don't understand is how to manage people, squads, good and bad times. That's where you suffer and struggle."

Naturally, as a young man, Dent doesn't think football is a young man's game but he does recognise that without dedication to football progress is hard to come by.

"I don't necessarily think football is a young man's game but I do think that to get into football as a coach, the same way as a player, you have to start early. The reason being, it's very difficult to get the experience and the exposure if you're not fully committed to the cause."

He also, like Rush, believes he had to lose some of his humanness at the start of his career. He doesn't like it, he doesn't believe it's right but he felt he, like many others, had no choice if wanted to work in that environment.

"In a high-performance environment coaches feel like they have to perform straight away. If they don't then the chances in their minds disappear. That pressure to get into a senior environment, beyond the glass ceiling, in the first phase has a big consequence on coaches... When you get opportunities like that the feeling is you have to deliver but you don't always get someone else's experience to help you, the opportunity to make mistakes or learn from them. You have to just succeed."

Success cannot be instant though, nor can it be the only thing that matters to an organisation. Sadly for some sports, that pure football focus is still expected. Rush talked about it and even though Dent has since come through it the entirety of his career is built from someone willing to do and be more football than anyone else.

This is not a uniquely English or football problem either. When Dent first went to Norway in 2011 he was told by an academy director of a top-flight club that they only recruited coaches in their low 20s because they wanted coaches that didn't have ties to other things, families, another job. They wanted that full commitment. They knew because young coaches wanted a foothold in the game they would stretch themselves beyond what they would usually do.

From a business perspective this makes total sense, but is the short-term gain worth it? Surely a long-term investment in someone's life and health would not only generate interest but also staying power. After all, in England it didn't take Dent long to realise that he was stuck.

"When I got my foot in the door in Norway, everything blossomed in a way I'd always hoped it would do in England," Dent recalls.

Indeed, his venture to Norway, how it happened and all the adventures that led to him now being head coach of Blink are worth telling. Not only because they remind so many coaches that much like players sometimes the best way to move forward is first to move out, but also because they show how someone recognised the price he had been asked to pay by football and actively fought against it before it got the better of him.

Dent's story is marvellously entertaining in a way that doesn't seem possible in football anymore. His first love was music, and he lights up when he tells me about how he used to be a talented saxophone player aged 16. Three years earlier came football, and only because someone told him to go in goal on holiday. After that, Dent went into coaching at university where he coached anyone he could. Eventually, like many coaches, he was working for a club's foundation charity, taking football into the community. And while doing this at Fulham Dent's life changed.

One summer, the one after Fulham made the Europa League final, Dent had two Norwegian boys in his training camp. Wary they might feel out of sorts in another country, Dent did his best to make sure they too could enjoy the session. The boys' father, Tommy, recognised this and told Dent if he was ever in Norway to look him up. Eventually, after a failed plan to travel down Europe and visit as many clubs as possible that saw Dent get just two responses (Bayern Munich and Werder Bremen) from 200 letters, he sent Tommy a message saying he was interested in coming to Norway. Three months went by and he heard no word but just before Christmas, Tommy said just let me know how long for and we'll fix up a programme. When Dent arrived, he realised Tommy had left out the foundation part and had just told everyone locally a coach from Premier League side Fulham was coming. A chance meeting and misunderstanding later, Dent arrived in Norway and the course of his life changed for good.

By the second trip, Dent had visited a host of Norwegian clubs, had cake with Henning Berg at Lillestrøm and spent an hour talking football with the Follo head coach (Tommy's local team, third division) in a tiny shed until the head coach got a call from his wife asking him when he was coming home. That connection at Follo led to Dent coaching at holiday camps and before long there was talk of the club expanding their youth set up to include an U14s side. With Dent having just graduated from Brunel with a sports science degree and faced with interviews at Boots, the timing was perfect. He was, as he told me, ready for an adventure.

Tom spent three years there, following the same cycle of going in January full of energy and enthusiasm, returning home for the summer and then back to Norway and leaning towards returning home to England for good before realising every time there was nothing there for him.

When Tom arrived, Follo were in the second division. They got relegated, went straight back up in 2014, and then went back down in 2015 in the most heartbreaking fashion. On the final day of the season there were seven teams that could all be relegated in two spaces. In recalling the story, Dent says he thinks that throughout the 90 minutes all seven of the teams were relegated at one point. Follo had to win away and they were leading 2-1 for a long part of the game. There were four minutes of added time. The opposition had a free kick outside of the box as the clock struck 93 minutes and 30 seconds. The free kick went wide and everyone on the Follo sidelines was celebrating. The keeper took the goal kick and Dent remembers everyone getting ready to jump for joy but the whistle didn't come: "The opposition win the header, go down our left side, cross it in and they send a header towards goal. As the clock ticks 30 seconds over the allotted added time, the header deflects off a defender and goes in."

As soon as Follo kicked off the referee blew his whistle. Follo had been relegated. "That was pretty brutal," Dent recalls.

That marked the end of an era. The head coach moved on and even though Tom had no other job in sight it felt right to leave. He was coaching the U16s that had been his U14s, as well as coaching the goalkeepers and doing all the football schools. He was doing three jobs in one and it was time to change that.

Dent turned his phone off for a holiday with his family in the Mediterranean. Afterwards, when he turned it back on he had five missed calls and four messages. A friend had just been given the manager's job in the third tier, (ironically at the same club Dent is now head coach of - Blink) and wanted Tom to join him as an assistant. Dent was unsure, and his mother was against the move, but he realised that aged 24 he had been offered the chance to be an assistant coach for a men's first team in a national league. For an Englishman these are the jobs that are so hard to come by, the step on the ladder that often hangs on the horizon but rarely comes any closer. He felt he had to take it, and so he did.

A month in, Norway's federation decided to change the league system. In 2016, they had four groups in the third tier and they decided to make it two. A brutal restructuring ensued. League winners were promoted, teams placed second to seventh stayed up and teams from eighth to 14th were relegated.

Despite good home form and an amazing cup run that included a third round win over Ole Gunnar Solskjær's Molde, Blink struggled. In September, Dent realised he couldn't handle senior football. "I was so about development and process, things I could control. The result, being the thing I couldn't control, really bothered me. Especially to the point where we were playing well and doing the right thing, but we would get punished on corners, counterattacks. It was difficult to reset myself every time. When we had it tough that was when I felt the most lonely and I thought I had to go home. I knew it wasn't about football, it was about me."

Dent said he would leave at the end of the season. A week later the manager was sacked, and Dent, in his own words, committed the cardinal sin of staying. It was a decision partly out of personal pride of not wanting to jump ship, but it was a decision that cost him that friendship. For Dent though, the adventure continued because a week after the end of the season, Bodø/Glimt called asking him to be their U16s coach. This was the first move in Dent's career where he made a conscious decision not to make football everything. "When I moved to Glimt I made a very conscious decision that I had to get a life outside of football."

As fate would have it, two weeks after starting at Glimt, Dent met his now fiancé, a by-product of the decision to choose life over football. He told me that once at University he had passed up a dinner with his flatmates to watch El Clasico, such were his cravings for football. In Glimt, he had gone to a quiz night with the club's social media manager, but the second week Dent was stood up yet decided to go on his own. That night he met his fiancé.

To begin with he still struggled because every time they met up, in his mind he was weighing up the games he was going to miss. After six months they went on a trip together and he opened up to her about that struggle: "I told her she had opened my eyes to the world, not just a round ball. I remember we both cried."

Dent spent four years at Glimt. He was the first foreign youth coach Bodo had ever appointed and eventually was made responsible for the development of teams and the coaches of those teams. But Dent found it hard coaching people twice his age - he was 27 and managing people who had been at the club for 15 years.

That brings us to two Christmases ago, when Dent realised that despite his best intentions to keep football at bay, balance was still elusive: "I just needed someone to talk to about what I was feeling and whether it was rational or irrational, and working out ways to split the day so that when I came home I was present, I was there. It wasn't just, I'm at home thinking about who I needed to speak to the following day and checking emails on my phone."

He spoke to a mental coach (educated as a sports psychologist) and years later is proud to talk about how he feels a more rounded person. He has taken up running, enjoys documentaries on historical events and turns off his phone more often now.

Dent has also transferred his learning into his coaching. He is willing to be vulnerable with his team. In April 2021, his uncle suffered a stroke and had a heart attack. Dent told the team before they went out to training that he wasn't in a good place. He didn't tell them why, but just let them know how he was feeling and that it had nothing to do with them. Dent believes there is no point in hiding anything, and in turn he has noticed his players are increasingly open with him as a result.

When he was younger, Dent never had the dream of becoming a top-level coach. He played football because he enjoyed it. He coached because he enjoyed it. Once in the coaching system though, he found himself institutionalised by this pressure to climb the ladder, to break the glass ceiling. He made it through but still suffered as a result from an environment that expects everything.

In expectation of everything that sport can sometimes lead to, people forget their enjoyment of it. Dent believes football misses this, youthful enjoyment over professional ambition. He diligently points out that while academies have had success, what does life actually feel like for those in them? Dent is back in control of his life and at 30 the paths ahead of him are endless, and no longer all football-related. I can't help but hope one of them might include the saxophone.

9

Norway

There is so much noise around performance in sport, but how much of it helps the person? Clearly, in sport performance matters and a sporting lens is not only necessary but also logical. And yet, performance in sport is often represented through a numerical value. Again, analysis is a necessary step and has enabled sport to move forward in many positive ways. But how often is the performance lens removed? As Rush and Dent mentioned in the previous chapter, there is often a price to pay for solely focussing on the sport.

Naturally, the presence of a mental coach allows athletes to develop skills that are also useful off the field, and that work can open the door for other areas of personal development. However, often these skills are still occurring inside the context of performance. They are all geared towards playing better, winning more. Even if the coach themselves has desires for that work to impact beyond their day-to-day life it is rare that that opportunity is given or available in such pressure-filled environments.

Given that the player is there to perform well and help their employer be successful, this seems justifiable. After all, to help them in any field that doesn't contribute to success would require justification. The question is, should it? Is it not logical that to consider the human being inside the athlete also needs consideration and care?

After all, our work does not occur in a vacuum. Who we are, how we live, how we feel matters, and will ultimately impact our performance. Again, these questions can and indeed often are handled effectively by the club's sport psychologists, but they too are still employed by the club and are battling with a performance lens.

Was it even possible for performance and personal development to truly coexist in high-performance environments? Once again I found an answer in Scandinavia.

Bjørn Mannsverk speaks slowly. It's not because his English is limited but because he chooses his words carefully. Given he is mental coach for Norwegian top-division side Bodø/Glimt it is not that surprising, but it is still impressive to listen to someone who doesn't waste words.

Four years after Mannsverk started working with Bodø, the club won their first ever Eliteserien title. Naturally that success came as a result of a combination of player quality, the right coaching and an adaptable, forward-thinking club philosophy.

There is no doubt though, that Mannsverk's work over time played a big role. In fact, an article in the *New York Times* at the end of 2020 about Bodø/Glimt's success includes quotes from players and coaches at the club that say the club's success would not have been possible without Mannsverk. This is just the latest proof that working on the minds of young athletes, in combination with the aforementioned factors, can lead to tangible success.

However, in the same *New York Times* article there was also a comment from Bodø midfielder Patrick Berg, where the young man stated that Mannsverk helped him as a player but also as a person. Performance had been the focus but the person had been included throughout. This was not just about developing better footballers but people better prepared for life during and after their sporting careers.

Mannsverk has worked hard in the familiar areas of identity, control and attention to help players. This is by no means revolutionary in the field, but it was his pursuit of helping players not just be players that struck a chord. After all, the decision to find contentment within the person whilst balancing the desire to improve as a player is not as common.

"You have to divide yourself into being a private person and playing football. I have confidence in playing football but self-esteem is more important. You should feel good, happy with yourself. I can still become better but I'm happy because I'm working hard, challenging myself, making mistakes, not focussed on others' opinions of me. You have to figure out the self," Mannsverk tells me during a call in the spring of 2021.

Outside of nutrition and sleep, the choice to be a footballer 24 hours a day, seven days a week is an unhealthy one.

"I approach it through the physical domain. Can you train all the time? What will happen to your body? Should you think about football all the time? Focus is important, being on and off. You should pick up a hobby, meet friends. It's really important to be really off because then you'll be back on on the pitch."

The connection to performance remains obvious and in many ways necessary, but it is in the details that Mannsverk's work on the person shines. The coupling of self confidence with playing time is very common, but in the simple phrasing of the question and giving the player time to consider, Mannsverk opens the door to a world not connected to corner flags and penalty boxes.

"I need to play to increase my self confidence, but that doesn't make sense. If you get injured, you can't play. When you stop playing, either because of injury or because you have reached the end of your career, what happens to your self confidence? Where are you in life?"

To handle the big questions Mannsverk helps the players lay the groundwork. They have developed a language around how to express feelings and emotions. This development over two years helped battle the stigma that still surrounds mental work. Most common is the idea that stepping into this area as a player is a sign of sickness or weakness. "I talk to really healthy people. It's a mystery for me that this isn't all over. This is low hanging fruit."

There's also the perception that Mannsverk's work is part of a soft model, as someone once told him. "The perception is that it's just nice to chat to players, but the truth is the talks are hard."

With the stigma removed, the perception changed and emotions out in the open, players were able to mature enough so that when Mannsverk introduced a performance focus in 2019, everyone was ready for it.

"There's a lot of people talking about performance in the world but for me they are not. They are missing the last step," Mannsverk says. "I am impressed with the language the Bodø/Glimt players use around performance."

He is also making strides. Ahead of a game week, Mannsverk heard someone say: "This team fits us well". With this simple sentence the expectation to win is planted, even if just subconsciously. Bringing attention to that is changing the language around the club, and in turn the way the club operates.

Without the support of the club, a strong connection with the head coach and buy-in from the players, Mannsverk's work would not have been possible let alone as successful. He was able to anchor himself with the leadership of the club, who wanted this approach and had a plan to implement it. Clubs who want to do this "need to support this with their heart."

Mannsverk was able to work freely. He was not an agent of the club. He was there for the people.

"If I challenge people and ask, 'Do you like football' and they say no then I will say then you should stop playing football. The club needed to take the risk because I have to keep my integrity."

The reason Bodø did that was because they knew they needed

mental training. They knew they needed something accepted and it was Mannsverk's background that got him the opportunity. "They said, 'If it works for a fighter pilot, it should work for a footballer.'"

After 20 years of active duty in Norway's air force, Mannsverk was well established in performance culture. He had lived the entire experience of being selected based on high motivation, physical and psychological strength and intelligence. He knew what it was to focus on becoming the best possible in your field. But then Mannsverk hit a turning point.

"Then you establish a private life, you get yourself a partner and kids. I ended up not having a balance. I was at work thinking I should be home and at work thinking I should be home."

His dream of being a fighter pilot was no fun anymore. "I had to figure it all out again. Why am I doing this? I needed to find balance, maybe lower my expectation as a fighter pilot and acknowledge that this was more than enough, that I was doing really fine."

With that acceptance, Mannsverk became more confident and more of a leader. He became deputy commander of the squadron and was responsible for training the next generation of fighter pilots. He saw them go through the same journey he had, the one that starts with an eagerness to get started and become the best, the one that is full of long days and endless effort, and the same one that eventually develops a private life, loses balance and sees frustration creep in. Mannsverk realised he could make a change to that cycle. And yet, despite younger recruits recognising they were struggling and agreeing on the lack of balance, they kept doing what they were doing.

He learned about visualisation and internal dialogue, but the light in his head switched on when he learned about mindfulness. This was the piece of the puzzle he had been missing. Mannsverk brought that into the squadron with the focus of helping each individual find out where they were and how they should prioritise their life. He ran the sessions for more than a year, just before the Libya project. He saw the effect it had on the pilots in a war zone.

And his continuation with that work, being a part of performance culture, understanding what to do on an individual and organisational level and truly understanding leadership through experience, is why Bodø called.

And, as with any turn in life, he had a decisive piece of fortune. The first player Mannsverk spoke to was planning on playing out the rest of the season and then leaving. Now he's one of the team captains. Players could see how much of a different Mannsverk's work could make. It solidified a bond of trust that has grown stronger ever since.

Once every three weeks, Mannsverk comes in to chat to players. Not every player wants to get involved and that is fine, but after speaking to head coach Kjetil Knutsen and the club's medical team he sits down with those who do want to chat. At the time we spoke in spring he recalls that during his last visit he spoke to 14 players, close to his limit. With each session lasting 30 minutes that meant he spent seven hours "beak to beak" before a one hour group session.

Thanks to the trust, support and time he was given, Mannsverk was able to build the group towards being increasingly self-sustained. "We have group sessions where the players share cases, challenges, experiences, they ask questions and are open-minded."

That means that when focus started to turn more towards results he was able to bring attention to the importance of performance with a foundation of trust already in place. It was less creating a performance culture but rather merging into one. The pieces were already there, the light just needed to be turned on.

During a preseason training camp in Spain, Mannsverk asked about the club's ambitions for the season ahead. The responses were typical: a points total, the number of wins or finishing in the top three. For Mannsverk, this didn't make sense.

"What about you just focus on the performance, and the players being the best versions of themselves?" He urged them to turn attention to team strength and loyalty to themselves. He wanted the club to disregard results.

"If we are supposed to learn by mistakes then we need to use every opportunity to learn from them. I have a feeling we focus on the mistakes when the results are bad. We don't when the results are good. I understood there is a lot of coincidence in football. I saw you won that game but you were lucky, or the other way around. You are missing a lot of learning opportunities. A performance culture is where you always learn, share and analyse how the performance is. Disregard the results

- they put a tag on performance."

Mannsverk welcomes mistakes because he knows that means players are not just playing within their comfort zone. He encourages clarity of focus when it comes to considering the decisions required to achieve goals. Again though, just when it feels like performance has cast personal development aside, Mannsverk finds a way to bring it back to the person.

"We are never happy, we can always get better but still we are happy with our own performance. It's a special situation. We're never happy, but at the same time we are happy but we can always be better which is a positive thing. It's a healthy approach."

He has made sure that the endless quest for sporting development is balanced with moments of contentment and acknowledgement that who you are and what you are doing is good and making you happy.

This work makes Mannsverk happy, and it's no surprise to hear that he sees working in academies as the future. "If I can see the guys in the A-team struggling then I know if I go back to where it all started and being 14, 15... We're going to introduce mental training as an integrated part of being in an academy. I think I lost a lot of talents because they were already gone."

Mannsverk's situation is unique. Remarkably, this work is the Norwegian's hobby - his full-time job is as a security advisor. In his context this is how he is able to do it best and retain balance. For others it won't be the same and clubs looking to do the same in this field must take that into consideration.

Mannsverk has had offers to do this work full time, but at the moment he wants to make sure he keeps his balance. Thanks to his own experiences, and many conversations with his wife, he is able to do that. That puts him in a great spot to help so many others. "These guys are really prepared for life after football," he says just before we say goodbye. The truth is, they're probably just as prepared for life during it as well.

10

North America

Simone Biles' decision not to participate for almost all of Tokyo 2020 to protect her mental health was largely met with supportive messages.

Biles, one of the most decorated Olympians of all time and one of the most remarkable gymnasts in history, made the decision for herself after suffering from the "twisties" - a frightening state of disassociation that often occurs while spinning in the air, preventing athletes from successfully completing a skill and making them far more prone to serious injury. After her Olympics were over, Biles also revealed that her aunt died unexpectedly during her time in Japan.

That Biles felt good enough to compete in the balance beam event is remarkable. That after that week and the years before as one of the gymnasts who was sexually abused by the USA Gymnastics' former doctor Larry Nassar she won bronze is quite extraordinary. "(The bronze) means more than all the golds because I've been through so much the last five years and the last week while I've even been here," Biles told American broadcaster *NBC* afterwards.

It was another significant move towards more consideration for the human being over the final results in professional sport and another reminder that athletes are not robots. That however much training they undergo, they can still be prone to the same moments of doubt and fear that we all face at one point or another.

Months before, Sha'Carri Richardson faced similar doubt and anxiety when, as former NBA player Etan Thomas wrote in *The Guardian*, her decision to use cannabis was essentially an "admission that she had self-medicated to cope with the death of her birth mother in the days before the US trials." That decision cost her a place on the US Olympic team. As Thomas eloquently put it, a situation like this needs more compassion, and hopefully a "reevaluation of the rule itself, but at least serve as a reminder to fans that athletes are in fact human beings."

Opting out in the middle of a competition and using cannabis to treat anxiety are two very different ways to handle mental health issues, but this difference is proof of how varied we are as people. There is no single template for us all to follow on how to heal and care for ourselves. Richardson broke the rules as an athlete (prompting a discussion about the wisdom of a cannabis ban), but did what she needed to do as a person. If sport is more interested in the former rather than the latter, then it will become increasingly unrecognisable as athletes are forced to become more and more robotic. This is perhaps not that surprising for an industry increasingly driven by profit. Sport is made by its numbers and so the pursuit of improving upon them and the numbers that fund them often come hand in hand.

Much of the world operates under a capitalist system, and nowhere is capitalism more pervasive in every aspect of life than America. Operating under the fallacy that in capitalism, anyone can realise any personal dream, the pursuit of profit hovers over the so-called 'land of opportunity' like smoke from a forest fire. Capitalism incentivises people to try to maximise their income through competition, and American sport is the perfect example of how to dive in at the deep end of competition for entertainment. Salary caps and the draft give a veneer of fairness to the field of play, but the money involved has grown exponentially and shows no signs of slowing.

One of the first costs of a system where people are looking to maximise profits to the exclusion of all else is the protection of the human being. Capitalism, which inherently amasses wealth for an increasingly small number of individuals, does nothing to promote equal opportunity. This leaves those without good health, support, or access to education (to name just a few factors) without a fair chance. People are being held back before they've even had the chance to compete.

The quest for profit is no different in professional sport, which is now so focussed on the business side it acts like Amazon; athletes are the products to be bought, consumed and discarded (i.e. traded) without much consideration for the person or the ecosystem in which they exist. Whether you're hitting balls out of the park in New York, dunking in Denver, scoring in Seattle, passing the puck in Pittsburgh or catching touchdowns in Tampa, players (and staff to a certain degree) are bounced around like commodities in an enormous and fluid stock market that is about numbers before nature.

Forbes' list of Most Valuable Sports Teams of 2021 is headed up by American football team the Dallas Cowboys, who are followed by baseball team New York Yankees and basketball team the New York Knicks. Only three of the top ten are not American teams. The NFL, the league the Cowboys play in, just agreed to extend their regular season by one game (17 + playoffs), while major league baseball teams play 162 games in a regular season (+ playoffs). Teams in the NBA play 82 games (+ playoffs). There is no shortage of competition in American sport, but with that in mind, and in the context of one of the world's most aggressively capitalist countries, how on earth can sports teams in the US proclaim to be invested in the human being?

In the National Football League (NFL), American football players have long spoken about their struggles. For example, the way painkillers are used as a way to deal with concussions. This illustrates how their physical health was less of a concern (and perhaps still is) than the bottom line, and therefore it is no surprise that mental health was a vanishingly small worry for team management. In previous eras awareness, proactivity and support were not what they are today - which is why people like Ricky Williams, the former Miami Dolphins running back, struggled with social anxiety.

"I was 23, a millionaire and had everything, yet I was never more unhappy in my life," Williams said in 2009 in an article published by the *Anxiety and Depression Association of America.*

In January 2020, after losing in the divisional playoffs, Seattle Seahawks running back Marshawn Lynch spoke openly about the importance of self-care:

"*So while y'all at it right now take care of y'all bodies, you know what I mean? Take care of y'all chicken [money], you feel me? Take care of y'all mentals, 'cause look, we ain't lasting that long. You know, I had a couple players who I played with that they're no longer here no more, they're no longer. You feel me? So start taking care of y'all mentals, y'all bodies and y'all chicken for when y'all ready to walk away. You'll walk away and you'll be able to do what you want to do.*"

On the surface, it looks like there is plenty of support on offer across the major sports in America. In 2019, the NFL agreed to incorporate mental and behavioural health into its programme by offering a behavioural health team clinician who will be available to players for a minimum of 8-12 hours per week. The league also has a mental health and wellness committee, with designated people creating structures to offer support in a variety of ways.

In the spring of 2021, the Indianapolis Colts launched 'Kicking The Stigma', an initiative to raise awareness about mental health issues and address the perceived shame associated with mental illness. The fundraiser alone raised $4.5 million and team players were vocal on the matter. This year, players in the league have continued to speak out about their personal struggles, such as Jacksonville Jaguar wide receiver DJ Chark, or Dallas Cowboy quarterback Dak Prescott.

NBA stars Dennis Rodman and later Allen Iverson both struggled mentally but, like the aforementioned NFL players, were both living during an era with much less awareness.

It was in that era though, that one of the most dominant and successful teams in sport ever played. The 1990s Chicago Bulls twice won three straight NBA championships, with the last one recently documented in the Netflix Series *The Last Dance*. In that series, Michael Jordan talked about winning and leadership having a price. This quote from Jordan in one of the last episodes generated a lot of interest, with many believing this to be one of the key secrets to winning.

"My mentality was to go out and win at any cost... If you don't want to live that regimented mentality, then you don't need to be alongside of me because I'm going to ridicule you until you get on the same level with me. And if you don't get on the same level, then it's going to be hell for you."

Some may argue, as Jordan does, this is the necessary mindset in order to win in high-performance sport but it remains intriguing that Jordan believes the path to victory lies with making someone else's life hell. Furthermore, what if winning at all costs includes the price of your own or other people's well-being? Is it worth it then?

Luc Longley, the seven foot, two inch Australian who played a key role in the Bulls' championship surge, was rarely featured in the Netflix show. The gentle giant didn't fit the bill, but an Australian Story special documentary series by ABC (*Luc Longley and the 'missing chapter' of the Last Dance*) later focussed on Longley's role in the iconic basketball team. In that series, Longley admitted that his quiet, empathetic nature didn't fit with the NBA and that ultimately he felt basketball "eroded" him as a person.

"I feel like basketball has given me an awful lot," Longley said on the series. "And it's also cost me a fair bit in a lot of ways. I had to change an awful lot of who I was in order to do the job and coming out of that I learned that not all of that suited me very well and it's taken me a long time to acknowledge that and

unpick it and I'm still unlearning."

Longley is not the man in the headlines or the one sinking the winning shot. As such, his experience is less discussed But perhaps it should be. Ultimately, a young man who never planned for basketball to be a big focus in his life became the most successful Australian man to play the sport of basketball because he was able to mould himself to what basketball and his teammates demanded of him. That he was able to leave that world, do so much work to get back to who he felt he was, find peace and, in the end, reconnect with basketball on his terms is both a testament to him and a reminder of just how much that level of sport so often demands of people.

In 2018, Kevin Love changed the conversation around mental health in the NBA when he revealed he was struggling with anxiety and depression. Love's decision to speak openly not only helped change attitudes towards seeing the person and not just the athlete in basketball, but also led to the creation of a fund in his name that is aimed at helping children struggling with mental health issues.

Like the NFL, the NBA also has a designated individual for this field. Dr William D Parham is the director of the mental health and wellness programme for the league. The Golden State Warriors, likely inspired by their holistic coach Steve Kerr, have both a player mentor coach and a director of player affairs and engagement. What is revealing about the Warrior's staff in those positions is that both are occupied by recently retired players - Brazilian Leandro Barbosa and American Shaun Livingston. Perhaps they are just jobs to get the pair into coaching, but given their time under Kerr it seems more likely that they are both carrying the torch of the holistic approach in their roles. They have gone from players who their coach saw as people and are now helping the next generation of players be recognised as people too.

The NHL appears a little thinner as a league on this matter, although some teams do have individual coaches dedicated towards mental training. The same is true of major league baseball, which is all the more intriguing given the sport's existential crisis as fan numbers and profits dwindle.

In 2019, Dave Zirin wrote in *The Nation* that major league baseball (MLB) was struggling to survive in terms of popularity due to the length of its games and the inaction of team owners, citing a poll by American analytics company Gallup that revealed only nine percent of people in America listed baseball as their favourite sport. America's most traditional sport has been slow to catch up with the fast pace and adaptive nature of other American sports.

Furthermore, the MLB does not have a salary cap, but rather a luxury tax that fines teams for exceeding the amount set by the league. This means big market teams can generate and spend more money than others, creating an uneven playing field.

In response, teams opt to develop young players through the draft and by leaning into the league's active trade market. In 2020, the Tampa Bay Rays fell just two games short of winning the World Series by following this approach. Months later, they traded one of their best players, Blake Snell, in exchange for three younger players and an experienced catcher. By the end of the 2021 season, the team with one of the lowest payrolls in baseball made the playoffs again, proving that finding value in the numbers was a feasible way to be successful.

This entire approach was inspired by Billy Beane, the former Oakland Athletics general manager. Beane's pivot to greater analytics revolutionised one of America's oldest sports. With a flood of data, it became easier to make more confident, evidence-based decisions about recruitment and opened the door for teams with a smaller payroll to find players who could contribute while not costing too much. The A's didn't win a World Series with this approach, but they exceeded expectations and went on a 20-game win streak (fifth longest of all time), which was enough to shake up baseball. The age of analytics was important for the sport, as it has been for other sports, but how far is too far when it comes to the numbers?

Regular roster upheaval already makes life harder for fans to form ties with a team that is always changing. Why invest in a whole if the parts are so rarely the same? There is no time for something to form, between the team and the community as well as inside the team. Furthermore, the trade-heavy approach also makes it harder to create an environment that considers the human being. All modern sports are businesses but must that come at the expense of an environment conducive to long-term human joy, effectivity or purpose?

There are some clubs who are doing it differently, thanks either to a change in club philosophy or to individuals who care about the human. They are recognising the need for more focus on the person, not only because there's a recognition that analytics alone cannot provide all the answers but also because there is a growing sense that looking after the person is both the right thing to do and the most sustainable way to live and to improve performance. And one of those teams plays major league baseball (MLB).

The Toronto Blue Jays are the only MLB team not from America, and intriguingly are one of only two MLB teams under corporate ownership. The Canadian club's glory days lie in the mid 1980s and early 1990s, but since then the quest for a championship has been a struggle. In 2001, the Blue Jays hired general manager JP Ricciardi, who had worked for Billy Beane at the A's, but any hope that lessons learned from the analytics revolution would benefit Toronto were washed away by inconsistency. The Blue Jays would go on a record run of 22 years without making the playoffs.

That ended in 2015, when the Blue Jays came within touching distance of the World Series. Not long afterwards, Mark Shapiro was named the new president, and a new general manager (GM), Ross Atkins, also arrived. An organisational shift occurred, and interestingly all four members of the leadership group used to work in farm teams, a colloquial term for a baseball club's system of affiliated minor league teams designed to develop talented players until they can contribute in the major leagues.

Shapiro might be the most intriguing of the group, and is proof of how important it is to have a human-focussed philosophy from the top down. He wants to build for the long term, hire people who embody the organisation's values, and create a culture where winning is the byproduct rather than the sole aim.

In 2002, back when Shapiro was GM of the Cleveland Indians, he was interviewed by Linda Feagler in the *Cleveland Magazine* just three months after Cleveland's season had ended (without a trip to the playoffs). What he said while on holiday and already thinking about next season says a lot about his philosophy, and supports the notion that the Blue Jays are truly an organisation doing it differently.

"*I believe the greatest fulfilment in winning comes from winning the right way... I want players who are motivated by pride and pride alone. Players we can believe in both as people and as talent... The core of my personal philosophy is to never let my job define my worth as a human being... I want my value as a human being to be governed by who I am as a husband, brother, son, father and friend."*

The first signs of this change were seen in 2019, when the Blue Jays improved the salary of their development players in the minor leagues. This decision came after minor league baseball players were exempted from a law which stated they were not entitled to a minimum wage and overtime pay. Many minor league players earn less than $10,000 a season (which lasts between April and August), with offseason training and team events not covered.

The Blue Jays decision to increase that income by 50 percent is not an enormous step but it does allow for players to live more comfortably, sleep better, eat healthier and not have to get an extra job in that time. This is direct action looking after the person, and can only lead to a better quality of life as well as more opportunities to improve performance in the ball park. The decision falls in line with an organisation that is looking to put the well-being of their players higher on the list of priorities. Pivotally they recognise this is just a first step, given that, amongst other possible avenues, there is still plenty of room to increase minor league salaries further.

The organisation has continued on that path, building a new player development complex in Dunedin, Florida, where the team has long held its spring training camp. Completion of this $100 million project was only possible with help from the city, county and state, taking some of the shine off the initiative.

In the current sports era of incredibly advanced facilities and gigantic stadia, the decision to invest in a player-development centre is not revolutionary, but the thought process behind it includes more areas that merge into human development. The new complex includes a movement studio for yoga, sports science labs, dining areas, classrooms, player lounges and even a barber shop. All of these additions are the creation of places in which human development can occur naturally. For many organisations this a first step. The next is having the right people in the building to put language to it.

Under a leadership group clearly more forward thinking, the Blue Jays appointed Ben Freakley as a mental performance coach in early 2017. Nearly two years later, Freakley was made head of mental performance at the organisation. His role is not unprecedented in sport and while a performance focus does not always translate to holistic development, Freakley's work is nonetheless encouraging.

He was part of and has now created a team of six who are there to help the person's performance through their mind. One of the team is a clinical mental health counsellor, a programme that Freakley and two colleagues are also training to be qualified in and that Freakley believes anyone working in mental health should consider. The six spread their work across the organisation, with some involved with the major league team while others focus on the minor league players and the development centre. This is where Freakley spends most of his time, working with those aiming to make it into the major leagues as well as those rehabilitating through an injury. He has established, with others in the organisation, a mental care approach from the moment players are signed or drafted all the way through their time at the organisation.

"If you look at our major league team right now, several of our players are homegrown guys, guys that we drafted and put in our developmental system and just allowed to flourish," Freakley explains on a call in late May 2021, before elaborating on how his work is integrated into the draft process.

"We are very curious about their support, who has been in their life, who has influenced them. We're curious about the type of teammate they are and what they care about in teammates. And even yesterday in the texts we were sending around, the very first priority was around really spending time with these players, messaging how important it is to be great teammates and have a collective care for this common mission of bringing a world championship back to Canada. In a pro sport environment, it's easy to look at some of your teammates as your competition. We really want to, as much as we can, promote this concept of lifting all boats."

Freakley is deeply enthusiastic about his work, and his voice bounces with infectious energy when he talks about what he calls the privilege of walking with someone for part of their journey. For someone working in performance he is refreshingly aware of the holistic element.

"One of our Blue Jays values, but also very much in line with a personal philosophy of mine, is collaborate. I love the phrase

'People are a lot more likely to commit to what they helped create.' Our mission is to support the mindset development of every player in this organisation. I think the word 'support' is critical because we have no ego or need to be the ones that are directly doing this."

Freakley and his team have recognised that their best way is through the coaches rather than stepping into the centre of the frame themselves. This is just one of the philosophies considered when designing "The Separator", a little black book created by conversations, experiences and research in sport and performance psychology that is the framework of how the Blue Jays work on the mind. The approach is a five pillar one.

"We model and teach the pillars of get tough, train to win, make an impact, be a pro and thrive," Freakley explains. "Tough framework is basically how we describe, define and talk about mental toughness, resilience, mentality, mindset. A lot of these words are interchangeable. They all have different meanings for us. We've collaborated with coaches, players, psychologists, and we came up with our 'Get Tough' framework."

While the name sounds a little too sharp for holistic development, Freakley and his team believe that toughness is connected to being present, living personal values and staying composed. Ultimately if someone is mentally tough then they are present.

"Our philosophy is that elite performers can regulate their attention and emotion under pressure in any circumstance," Freakley explains. "Most of our work would lend itself to the pressures that the game brings and how attention and emotion are critical for performing under pressure. However, you and I know that it's not just the game that adds pressure. It doesn't have to be performance-related."

That is pivotal. The decision to recognise the human is a huge step towards holistic development. Freakley knows that pressure can also be raising a family or being a good partner or son or daughter, and that is where the thriving aspect of Freakley's approach comes to the fore.

"We think somebody who's mentally tough can be present. They can let go of any distracting thoughts. They can be clear on what their personal values are. What would kindness look like in this moment? What would perseverance look like in this moment? What would calmness look like in this moment? That's really a lot of where the 'thrive' chapter comes into play, where concepts like optimism, gratitude, resilience and mission are discussed. What's your mission and how does baseball help you fulfil that life's mission? And that's a journey for a guy to go on."

There is evidently more to a player than who he is on the mound and it is clear that the Blue Jays have recognised that. This organisation delivers education around Blue Jays culture, what it means to be a teammate, how they practice as well as introducing new signings to all of the team's resources. Again, this is not revolutionary and it won't be done by everyone but it is also not something every team offers. Putting a framework together around what it is to be a Blue Jay and how that is transferred into everyday life takes time and effort, especially if you want it to feel genuine.

"What happens in a culture when the technical staff spend as much time designing culture programmes, well-being programmes, care programmes as they do designing training sessions that they'll dedicate hours to? How are we going to deal with this player? How are we going to deal with that player? We'll spend hours doing that, and we're serving the team, we're serving results, we're serving performance. But for me, this is all about what are the ways that we measure success. Winning is one of those ways. Development is one of those ways, but so are thriving and well-being. People showing up to work where they feel like they can be themselves, where they feel like they're supported. Several coaches and I were talking about this yesterday, the idea of a high sense of ownership. I know a lot of people in my field do a lot of study around self determination and how predictors of autonomy and competence and relatedness are such critical components of motivation. When those things are dripped into an environment, we can ask how can we give players more choice? How can we create more moments of belonging? How can we create more mastery experiences? Thinking about those things really excites me and those are conversations I love being a part of."

Freakley's admission that these are conversations already being had inside the organisation is hugely encouraging. The Blue Jays have acted on and invested in human development, without doing much talking about it either. Aided by a department that does not feel the need to shout from the rooftops about their work, the work itself can take centre stage. This is also encouraging because the basis of positive and genuine human development is to do it for the joy of helping others, not the appreciation or applause that can accompany it. Ego is removed and while sporting performance is still a large focus, there is at least a significant element of human focus included.

"One of the things I just love about being a Blue Jay is I really feel that there is a universal commitment to the holistic development all the way down from our players in the Dominican Republic," Freakley says, referring to the club's two lowest level minor league teams, both of which are based in the Dominican Summer League in the Dominican Republic. "This is more than just pitching, hitting and base running. We really want to equip these young men at every turn and know that we can provide resources to them at a very high level."

With the facilities on offer and Freakley and his team so tapped in to all sides of athlete life - aided further by Freakley's work outside of sport that aids perspective in a field that often struggles to view itself out of its own context - concerns around a performance-focussed mental training approach were quietened. But is the reality inside the atmosphere of a high-level baseball organisation different? Freakley admits he and his team will not turn off a relentless mindset if an athlete arrives with one but they will focus on the fine line in between ruthlessness and unhealthiness.

"One of the things that we talk quite frequently about is the difference between reflecting and ruminating," Freakley explains. "You know, the player that cannot let go, the player that dwells on the last performance, the player that ruminates and just constantly listens to the inner critic... if we had the trust and relationship of that player we would want to maybe teach him some different ways to reflect on performance. And we have some different models and processes that we use that I think can help players get from ruminating, dwelling, and the tension, anxiousness and frustration that come with that, to moving into a reflective practice that can be done more objectively, that allows a player to step back and analyse the whole performance, not just the moments when things were poor."

Here Freakley even cites the same idea that Stephen Rollnick spoke of, that his job is more than to be a deficit detective. Mental training does not always need to be the quest to fix something. It can also be working on strengths.

"I talked to one of our coaches yesterday who had made it to a pretty high level and he was told along the way by a coach, 'Hey, that pitch you throw, don't throw it anymore.' And up to that point in his career, he considered that to be his best weapon. He said okay and stopped throwing it and he never found that pitch again. Along his journey, that was a very sad but defining moment. Sometimes when we are just looking at what's not working, what has to be better, we might forget that we have some incredible strengths. We might forget that there are some things that have brought us this far, and it's about how we balance both. I think that's an art. If it's just focussing on strengths, we may not reach whatever potential is in line for us. And conversely, if it's just focussing on weaknesses, constantly pressing and looking for exhortations and the next goal and the next outcome, then how much of our life do we really get to live? How much of it can we really be present for? And that's a very delicate balance that has to be done as a true partnership with the player because when a player comes in and they have an idea of or a recipe for what it's going to take to get to the top, you certainly don't want to slow them down. And at the same time, you don't want them to slow themselves down by constantly looking back and just living under this umbrella of 'it's not good enough, it has to be better.' I think coming alongside and saying: 'What is good enough? What is excellence? What is your standard, and if you don't meet that, at what point are you punishing yourself for that? How do you know when looking back is actually helping you? And at what times might that actually get into making it worse?' They have to explore that for themselves."

The reason Freakley and his team can do this is because they have invested time into their relationships, have tried to listen rather than fix and ultimately recognised and leaned into the fact that the players are the experts on themselves. Perhaps most important though, is Freakley's recognition that too much structure around this work can be prohibitive.

"I think the biggest change is when I came on, our programming was more structured, more on the schedule. We have found that promoting autonomy, and the more things that have been offered as optional leaves players over time seeking that growth. During spring training, we offered optional sessions for players and I was very encouraged by the numbers that showed up of their own accord. People see us as a group of coaches that are always going to be available, but also treat you as the expert. If you would like to come and meet with us, talk with us, you're going to get a listener, and an encourager too. We spend a lot of time talking about how we see ourselves as coaches, as threading or balancing the relationship between care and challenge. If they only get all care from us, there's no growth. And if they only get challenged by us..."

The area Freakley wants to improve on the most is helping players transition out of sports, a familiar issue across most sports. As we have heard in other chapters, the one question no one wants to answer is who is in charge of someone once they stop playing? Freakley doesn't have all the answers but he has recognised that to leave professional sport is also to lose a part of yourself and that needs to be remembered more often.

"I do some intern work at a hospice facility and when someone has experienced loss, we follow them for 13 months after that loss. Thirteen months, once a week, once every other week - there's availability all the way. I'd love to see more support and more resources and more programmes for athletes that are transitioning to the next phase where they can find that sense of identity, where they can find that sense of purpose, where they can find that sense of team... So much around athlete identity is 'I am number seven.' It can absolutely feel like a loss. It is a loss. I've talked with coaches here about that, that one day you're in the game, one day you're out and the game just keeps moving on."

Given there are 162 games in a regular MLB season, it feels like baseball is always moving on, but thanks to the organisational shift at the Blue Jays that recognised the importance of human development and the day-to-day work done by Freakley and his team, they are a team moving forward in a different way than just rolling through the schedule.

This approach takes time to bear fruit but they have got to work. They are by no means alone. Many American sports teams are recognising more and more that there is a person behind the performance, and that to care for them properly is to put structure and action to the words that so easily tumble out of the mouths of leaders. The leaders who have done both, as well as the work of smart and curious people in the field of human development and a general increase in societal awareness, have all contributed to sports teams being in this moment. The work has begun, the conversations are being had. Ultimately the hope is that Sha'Carri Richardson, Simone Biles or the next baseball player for the Toronto Blue Jays that needs more than just performance has the right environment and people around them to feel safe as a person.

11

Oakland

Oakland is one of the most ethnically diverse and liberal cities in America. It has a huge art and music scene and is the birthplace of MC Hammer, Mahershala Ali and Seasick Steve. Tupac Shakur lived there, Bobby Seale, activist and co-founder of the Black Panther Party, ran for mayor in the city, and there's a host of NBA greats who hailed from or grew up in Oakland.

Most major American cities boast a range of activists, athletes and actors, but there is something deeply interconnected about Oakland. Its people have withstood redlining - a discriminatory practice that puts services, financial and otherwise, out of reach for residents of certain areas based on race or ethnicity - to become a major force in the movement that led to the creation of the Civil Rights Act. It has struggled with drugs and crime, fought for its communities and against institutional racism. In 2012, the *New York Times* called the city the last refuge of radical America. For a city of nearly half a million people, it feels bigger than it is. Perhaps that's because it has spent so long overcoming obstacles many thought it couldn't.

And out of this swiftly changing and gentrifying city came Oakland Roots, a soccer team founded in 2018 who play in the Pacific Division of the USL Championship, the league below the MLS.

Former NFL great Marshawn Lynch is a part of the ownership group. The Oakland native decided to get involved after most of the city's sports teams had left, and because he has the chance to work with a local company to help Bay Area students with financial literacy.

"Giving kids in my home town a pro soccer club and players to look up to and a team that this community and city can get hella excited about was something I had to get down with," Lynch said in a statement. "And then, you layer in the commitment they are making to this city through all our grassroots efforts, the partnership with Goalsetter, just reassured and told me that the organisation isn't just talking about creating change, but really being about that action and making (stuff) happen."

Lynch's reassurance that the Roots were not just another sporting organisation talking about change but rather one enabling it highlights the truth about this team. The deeply personal nature of the Roots' reason for existence is a big part of why anyone currently involved never has to worry about a loss of humanity.

The club has a host of partners connected to purpose, such as Soccer Without Borders, a collective that looks after immigrant refugees and provides education and soccer mentorship. With the help of Matthew Wolff, the graphic designer who developed the popular 2018 Nigeria national team kit, the Roots created a brand for the club that was big and colourful. This personalised and community relevant merchandise that is available in an array of languages helped establish the club well beyond the football world. The Roots also have a community advisory board in order to maintain a continuous exchange with other sectors in the city and make sure whatever they want to do is done in a way that also best helps Oakland. Home games are less of just an afternoon of sport and more a festival of culture that involves local artists, musicians and service providers. As Luis Ruano wrote in an article for *Hypebeast:* “Many who have had the privilege of seeing the team live would agree that a Roots game feels less like soccer and more of a block party where anyone and everyone is invited.”

The club’s ethos is "Oakland first and always” and it is clear the Roots have grown through their community rather than away from it. This is the environment in which Roots players live. Shut up and dribble does not exist here; players are encouraged to speak their minds on issues facing the community.

In mid-March, the club launched a program called “Nurtured Roots” which focuses on both performance and purpose, encouraging athletes to consider nutrition and sleep as much as creativity, racial and gender equity, and self-expression. The program was born as a result of discussions about how the club could best support the players during the movement for racial justice that spread across the US in 2020, when Black Lives Matter protests were reignited by the murder of George Floyd.

Roots Assistant Coach Nana Attakora is quoted on the club’s website saying that: “It’s important to develop athletes in ways where they are prepared just as much off the field as they are on it, and to assist them in finding their identity and purpose outside soccer. We often look at athletes as strictly performers in the moment, and forget that they still have their whole lives in front of them after their short careers are over.”

There is great power in these words, but even more in the actions that accompany them. That a professional sports club is encouraging personal development alongside performance related goals is refreshing. Offering purpose-driven themes, topics for life after their careers such as financial literacy, and engaging in community partnerships and activities like scavenger hunts in order to learn more about the city (the winner gets to donate to their charity of choice), is to truly see your players as people.

To recognise the person in such a way is special in the context of high-performance careers, and any organisation doing something out of the ordinary requires extraordinary people. Lisa Bonta Sumii, a licensed clinical social worker who is also the club's first ever mental health and sports performance specialist, and Jordan Ferrell, the technical director and head coach, are exactly that. They speak with pride about the Roots, but also with conviction that this is the right way to do it.

"If you listen and look back at the history of the Roots and their rise, you can see that it comes from treating the athlete as a human," Bonta Sumii tells me on a call midway through 2021. "And when it comes top down, you know, it's supported. I know we have big, big dreams and hopes and visions for where this team can go on so many levels in our community, into the MLS. It's a matter of time because we're doing it correctly."

For Ferrell, an environment in which humans are allowed to personally develop is not only a necessity, but also a natural step forward in the time we live in.

"It has to be our environment," Ferrell says. "It's difficult. You have twenty, twenty-five different personalities in a locker room and all levels of alpha to omega and everything in between, even more so I think in our environment because of the diversity. People maybe try to communicate a little bit more or think about communication a little bit differently and so we have to think about the environment we create. I think we've put a lot of thought into not just the mental health, but also the other skills, career planning, financial planning, thinking about different ways in which they can use their platform as athletes to impact the environment. And then they find the environment around them and then they find an interest. So whether its climate change or voter suppression, education reform, all those things can speak to the interests of different people. It might bring out a part of their human that we wouldn't see if we focused only on the player."

That is not to say the Roots don't focus on performance, but given the club is closer to the bottom of the professional playing pyramid in the US, creating an environment that players really want to be a part of makes a lot of sense. If financial incentives are the deciding factor at the top level of modern football, then personal, emotional factors become even more decisive lower down the ladder. The club, though, has to find the right balance.

"Top players wanted to join but they weren't the right fit for what the club stands for," Ferrell says. "Who you are matters, but not to the point where that is the only focus. When we're recruiting, we say we always want ambitious people because if that's inherent you can tell if a player has the desire and drive to win a championship. You can also tell if a player wants to have an impact on the world around them. I like them as a person and I think they would be great here, and are they going to help us win?"

Winning is not something the Roots have done much of in their early years. However, focusing on what the club is there for gives them a much greater chance of long-term success. Appropriately for the location, there is an element of Bill Walsh's philosophy here. The former legendary NFL coach of the San Francisco 49ers lived the belief that faith in people meant the score would take care of itself.

While it is undeniable that the infancy of the Roots and its small size make it easier to choose culture over results, something which Ferrell acknowledges, the conscious decision to put the community of Oakland, its people and businesses first has been formative in the club's creation. This also makes for a far more personal experience for all involved.

The Roots defining moment on the field will come the day results pick up. Their club's values are at the top of the podium right now, but will they still be should the Roots become an MLS team one day? Will they still retain their community connection and holistic approach when the sums on the table are bigger, the pressure and expectations are greater and the noise around the club is much louder?

"It always comes back to your core values," Ferrell says. "If you stray from those you might have some results for a little while, but you're not going to achieve the same level. So if you define your core values really well and then you build around those... The purpose is the top... That's why I'm here. Working in football someplace else could be attractive, but this is one of those places where everything I know about humans, everything I know about the impact football can have, it's all here. There's a blank canvas to build it, so it's on us, but it is also the greatest opportunity."

Bonta Sumii joined the Roots for the same reason. She is proud to be a part of an organisation that cares about the person, the player and the community. Given her background in clinical social work and therapy in Oakland, and 20 years of working to help people heal from interpersonal trauma and community violence, focus on mental health and develop healthy relationships, Bonta Sumii certainly didn't need to join the Roots. But she was inspired to do so because this was not a team interested in commodifying their athletes.

"I was a soccer player all my life from age eight to 17, I got injured and my dreams to play collegiately and beyond, were totally smashed," Bonta Sumii says. "I didn't have support, physically or emotionally, so my purpose is to be able to give what I never received. And the fact that I'm a social worker means a lot to me, in becoming a part of the Roots family, because it involves community activism and multiculturalism. The way it marries for me and makes the most sense with the Roots is that their mission and purpose is the mission purpose of me as a human and in my profession. So, why not come together? Why not amplify this? Why not provide the support?"

Bonta Sumii provides just that, but she also helps the club understand what mental health is and how the club is going to talk about it. She looks for ways to make sure players don't change how they feel about themselves based solely on performance. On the surface, this is not uncommon practice in sports teams, but Bonta Sumii is able to thrive in this environment because everyone in the organisation believes in her work. As she mentioned earlier, their missions are connected.

"A lot of our guys come from all corners of the world, all different kinds of experiences, all cultures, religions, ethnicities, and so everyone has a different experience of what trauma means to them and how they processed it or not. And so just being able to let them know that this team values that and that we're a family and we're here to talk about that as much or as little as they want is super important."

Greater comprehension of that can lead to a clearer understanding of what matters to you as a person, as Ferrell explains using legendary American sprinter Tommie Smith, who won the gold medal in the 200 meter dash at the 1968 Mexico City Olympics.

"You can be at the pinnacle of the sport," Ferrell says. "Tommie Smith was the best 200 meter runner in the world and he used his platform to call attention to a lot of different injustices. That for me, that's the connection between the human and the athlete, one that utilises that platform. It's a really good way to say you can champion both."

It doesn't have to be activism, but clearly in Oakland, representation and using your platform for the community is more likely to play a key role. To reach that level of realisation is to take strides in personal development. To want to stand up for something you have to know what matters to you.

This is exactly what personal development should be about. It does not require a prescribed or regimented approach, but rather something specific to the person, location and time. Creating more space to look at the person is not to make everyone follow the same line, but rather give people the chance to develop into the person they want to be, whilst also retaining the values of the club.

In *The Captain Class*, Sam Walker explores the idea that the most effective leaders in sport do not always conform to expectation. These characters push boundaries as far as possible. Have these characters lost some of their humanity in exchange for a rare streak of competitiveness, or is it possible to balance the two? For Ferrell, the answer as to whether the cost of that competitiveness is too great is the real challenge for organisations like Oakland, whose foundation is built off caring about the person.

"I do feel like you need some of the grit, quality and intensity of effort. I don't know if you need the nasty," Ferrell says. "I think that that's the really interesting line, right? Sam Walker talks about this and I think that's a really good example of the best captains. They know the line between what's wrong and right. They work referees. They know what is wrong and right, and they keep their team focused on the right. That's the environment these captains create, so they can create that championship mentality. But as everybody knows, if there's a line it's going to get crossed at a certain point and that's something you have to accept. You have to be focused on having an environment that is highly competitive, but the right type of competitive."

Ferrell's acceptance that the line will be crossed at some point is recognition of the reality of competitive sport as it exists now. But just because a line is regularly crossed doesn't make it correct, or inevitable, and that is why the right kind of competitive environment is decisive. History will remember the winners, but people will remember those who won for their team, community, and ultimately the sport itself. To ignore personal development is to shut out that possibility, and to miss that even in highly competitive environments, the person plays a big role in determining the performance of the player.

"The output should be performance, and also their development as a human being, because this is going to be a part of what they do," Ferrell explains. "I think that's why we look at the way we look at the person, but the person within the environment, the context that they're interacting with and the variety of the environments that they are within because they're not just sitting in the one within the club and the one within the team. Everyone has history, everyone has something they bring and everyone has other social networks they're attached to that are making up that human being and who they are."

And for anyone connected to the Roots, a big part of forming who they are comes through being part of the city of Oakland. Ferrell went to school close to the city. His brother lived here. Bonta Sumii has spent decades working with people in the area. They know where Oakland sits in the environment of the Bay Area, the adjacent communities, the extreme affluence and extreme poverty that is scattered across the city. They know what Oakland is about and they, along with many other people around the club, make sure players know it too.

"This sets the stage for them to have a connection to what Oakland is about, the history of Oakland, the social justice history here," Bonta Sumii says. "There's so much that Oakland has experienced and it has produced so many great humans who are leaders in the social justice movement and across cultures... The guys feel more and more comfortable, open, and excited about doing the community service work alongside some of our partners in the community. The guys can join in some of the initiatives and projects going on in Oakland, get their elbows greased and be in there and act on our presence, not just be someone on social media. That's what we're about. It's so inspiring and awesome to see, and it's great the world can see it. It's great that people can see how special we are. I don't want us to be special for long. I want this to be what everyone does."

Not everyone can do what the Roots are doing, because no city is like another. What the Roots do is unique to them and their location and circumstance, but they are another example of an organisation that has recognised the person. They are proof it is possible.

"The Roots as an organisation help encourage and aid the players in finding their purpose and identifying their values so that no matter where we might go as a unit, a team, or a human, we are able to go back and refer to that and ask is this decision I'm about to make aligned with myself, my team, Oakland," Bonta Sumii says, poignantly.

What Oakland are doing is not that far away from what most major European football clubs once did. They were a representation of the community in which they played. They exemplified values and identities that connected the people, place and team. Now, the excessive profits, spending and hyper-professionalisation of the sport has seen many major European clubs completely lose touch with their origins. It is much harder to define what many modern clubs stand for, who they represent and what, if there is one at all, their purpose is beyond winning games and making money. For many watching on, this makes for a far more hollow experience.

The Roots' task in sealing that connection was undoubtedly made easier by being a new club. For clubs already well-established and steeped in history, this is much harder. There are more moving parts and the baggage of history weighs heavy, but it is still worth highlighting that the Roots didn't have to do it this way. The choice to make human beings and their community the foundation of the club is a deliberate one. Personal development at the Roots is guided on an individual level by the experience and knowledge of Bonta Sumii. It is integrated into coaching and the sporting environment by Ferrell and his staff. But it is the city of Oakland that provides the Roots with the greatest vehicle to personal development. Being here means much more than winning games. It's about being a part of something bigger than yourself.

12

Progress?

Despite having played roughly 30 years apart, Chris Ramsey and Marvin Sordell answered with a resounding and saddening no when asked if ever they felt supported as people during their professional playing careers.

"Not really," Sordell, who earned a three million pound move in January 2012 to then Premier League club Bolton Wanderers before finishing his career with over 300 professional appearances, including games for England's U21s and Team GB at the Olympics, says on a call during the summer of 2021. "Well, I say not really to be kind, but to be very frank, no. I think in football, players are very much treated as perks. You're as good as your performance. If you can't perform, you're not useful to the football club. It's as simple as a product, as simple as a pen. You buy the pen and use the pen. You expect it to be a pen that works and if it stops working and isn't doing what it's supposed to be doing then you chuck it out and get a new pen."

Ramsey, who spent most of his playing career at Swindon Town but was also a part of the Brighton and Hove Albion team that made the 1983 FA Cup Final, was equally as blunt.

"Not really... Along the way people did, but generally, no. I think we really have gone too far the other way [now] because I don't think we really prepare people for overall life," says Ramsey, who spent a decade coaching at Tottenham Hotspur before moving to Queens Park Rangers (QPR) in 2014, where he is currently technical director. "We've just done a big rotating release initiative over the last couple of weeks and a lot of it is heartbreaking because a lot of the kids have been there since they were six years old and they get released at maybe 19. That's all they know, so they become institutionalised. That in itself has not been the best because it's always an emotional time and breaking the news to parents and players is never enjoyable."

Despite playing in the modern era, Sordell suffered from a lack of support during his playing time and retired at 28 after recognising his happiness lay outside the game at that point. Since then, he has gone on to help others and tell stories through his videos that are helping to change the discourse around mental health.

Ramsey played football in the 1980s, a time when the concept of the person had little to do with the player. Still in football today, Ramsey sees the human impact of academy life and modern football almost every day. Both perspectives and experiences vary across the arch of human development, but both serve as reminders of the deeper, long-standing issues that sport and society still face.

Chris Ramsey's life is all about variation, the origins of which lie in the era he played in. In the 1980s, the hyper-professionalism, financial incentive and invasive marketing of the modern era did not exist. Football was exciting, but it wasn't as life changing as today. The life of a professional footballer was less regimented than it is today and that meant more opportunities to explore the world outside of football. And that is what Ramsey did. He worked in a recording studio and ran events, experiences that, perhaps subconsciously, changed him forever. Those decisions have impacted how Ramsey coaches and recruits other coaches today.

"When I started my journey in coaching, I didn't just want to be just a coach. I wanted to understand about physiotherapy so I went and did a diploma in that. I qualified myself in sports massage, aromatherapy, nutrition, weight training - all those sorts of things," said Ramsey, who has two degrees, one masters and multiple diplomas. "I wanted to really know the whole industry. First of all, because you can use them outside of football and secondly, it means that you're not just worrying about 4-4-2 or 2-3-5 and all that. You've actually got another string to your bow."

There is much more to Chris Ramsey than just an experienced coach. He knows much of the world outside of football and while that helps him be a great coach it also helps him live a fuller life. Furthermore, Ramsey's broad expanse of knowledge also allows him to spot people trying to bluff their way through a subject, a particularly useful trait in a sport so many are desperate to be a part of. "I may not be the expert on all the things but I'm going to know if you're not," he says with a wry smile.

A life of varied experiences combined with a desire to know more has also impacted Ramsey's handling of the next generation. Ramsey had to figure out it out for himself during his playing days but now he knows that the aspiration to be a footballer requires explorations into other parts of life, other parts of identity. "Sometimes when I talk to the kids now, I'm saying, 'Well, what do you know about this phase of history, what do you know about how films are made?' I tell them to do something that isn't just about football because they've got enough time to actually do it."

Beyond that lies the uncomfortable truth that for most young players in academies a job at the top end of the game is extraordinarily rare. In 2015, Alistair Magowan wrote an article for *BBC Sport* stating that only 0.5% of U9s at top clubs were likely to make the first team. In 2018, Michael Calvin wrote *No Hunger in Paradise*, a book investigating youth football in the UK that explored the sobering statistic that 0.012 percent of all the young boys who play organised youth football in England became a Premier League professional. Given the fluid nature of football and academies, that number is constantly changing but certainly not increasing exponentially. The stark reality remains the same, and it is in this environment that Ramsey is trying to create a culture at QPR where people are competitive but also aware of the value of learning and exploring a world outside of football. By assembling a diverse and qualified staff and delivering clarity to coaches about playing style, and youngsters about becoming first-team players, Ramsey has created a disciplined academy that speaks for itself. On the field, for the last three years, QPR have been in the top three in their league for academy minutes (playing time handed to players). Off it, they've had players go to Harvard, Swarthmore and Loughborough. Both are not guaranteed markers of human development or abnormal procedures in such environments but they are insights into the complexity of the work and why finding balance is so difficult. Parental expectation, competition against other clubs in London and the pressures that come with delivering players to the first team, against the aforementioned overwhelming odds, make maintaining a culture of both sporting and human development much harder.

"I think we have to do more to educate parents, because if you are in football you're always going to think that you're the one that's going to make it," Ramsey explains. "I think we have to manage the expectations of the parents better and get the parents more educated to manage the expectations of the child because the parents live vicariously through the kids and that is where the problem lies. You don't want people to be half- hearted about trying to make it the other end but you want to make sure that they realise you're not born a footballer, you're born a person and football is just an option for what basically is a vocation at the end of the day... Hundreds and hundreds and hundreds fall away emotionally by the wayside so I think we need to do better as an industry."

Ramsey has a firm approach to his coaching. He doesn't want coaches for their ideas, unless those ideas contribute to the philosophy already in place. He wants people who are the right fit for the club. Beyond the firm and fair approach lies a childhood full of truths that much of professional football has lost. Ramsey believes that training four times a week and going in regularly is such a life commitment for young players. He doesn't have all the answers, and saying as much is a sign of strength, but he does fondly remember his youth, when his commitment to football was present but without excess structure or professionalisation. It was organic and built around friends and play. Clubs like AIK are showing that such approaches can still exist in the professional world today, but the way Ramsey talks about playing with his friends in the park is a reminder that too much of youth sport is resigned to the history books.

"We were playing after school, in the playground, in parks. It was unsolicited training but we were playing all the time. And we used to walk to school, which was two miles away - that's four miles of just walking a day. And then you get to school, you play in the playground before lessons started, then you'd have a break, you play, then you'd play at lunchtime and after school. So you'd be playing three, four times a day. And then if you had the opportunity to you'd play for your school team on a Saturday and your Sunday team the next day or sometimes you'd play for the district. Then you'd have a midweek team to play for. In a week, I would say you're probably playing no less than three 11-a-side matches. And you wouldn't be saying at lunchtime: 'I'm not playing because I've got a district game on the weekend.' Before, people just played, you know. We look at it now and we say what dynamic stretching needs doing but when you've just done double maths and you're going down to the playground, you never see any kids stretching," says Ramsey, who of course acknowledges the importance of stretching but is simply showing that a simpler approach, especially with younger children, makes more sense. "We have to be careful how much we professionalise the kids early on."

Ramsey does his best to retain this organic play but inside a professional environment it's almost impossible, partly because of the environment but also because of the aforementioned parental expectation. Professionalism is what they sign up for and so the idea of saying to the kids, 'Here are the bibs, there are the balls, go and play' isn't exactly what parents expect from professional clubs.

Education though, is an expectation. While some may believe all football, all the time is the answer there are many parents who are distinctly aware of the slim chances of progressing to a sustainable, professional level and so are deeply interested in what clubs offer when it comes to education. While the league in England offers BTECs (specialist work-related qualifications), Ramsey has recognised that, unsurprisingly, a blanket approach doesn't work. He wants to support players to do what they want to do.

"A lot of the players who have got more strings to their bow probably need a different course so we've allowed that to happen and try to support them so it doesn't mean they can't do the football and their courses. I think vocational courses are probably as important as doing the more academic courses, because it means if someone doesn't make it they can just go straight into a job and they don't have to take a further course in something else or go to university. They can literally go and be an electrician or a plumber or whatever it may be. I think that would be a more sensible approach to try to help people vocationally rather than just pushing them towards the university," Ramsey says, before astutely pointing out that higher education is indeed not for everyone.

Educational support is hugely important in an industry that rarely if ever considers the needs of those who don't make the professional, first-team level. While human development will naturally occur through the learning of such skills, the provision of educational courses in a football academy is more human consideration than direct human development, a concept that extends through but also beyond the classroom. Granted, for some clubs merely considering the human would be a huge step in the right direction but do clubs like QPR have the time and resources to focus more on people and less on players? For Ramsey, the question is the wrong way round.

"We will develop players, the byproduct of that is we will develop people. The reality is you can have the best people but if you don't produce players you're not going to be in a job long," Ramsey says. He recognises that if an academy was built for a different purpose, such as The Right to Dream academy at Nordsjælland, then the focus can be flipped around and developing good people will lead to the development of players. For Ramsey, and the majority of others working inside financial pressure cookers like English football, the reality is that the owner of the football club is spending millions of pounds a year on an academy and expects results in the form of players merging into the first team. The rest falls into the 'nice to have' category.

It is hopeful to expect human development to progress in professional academies created for the sole purpose of delivering players to the first team, even with someone like Chris Ramsey involved. There are aspects of progress though that are deeply connected to human development and should be a given but sadly are not. One of those is a diversity. Learning from one another and living and working together with people from different countries, aware of different cultures, following different religions is a positive. Sadly, for Chris the battles he faces today as a black man coaching in England are the same ones he faced 20 years ago.

"I'm not really tired of talking about it because if you don't nothing changes, and you have to talk if you've got a platform, I think. A lot of times people don't realise that we're talking about the same thing 20 years on. There's been progress, but it's a long time for a little progress. It's not like it's a long time and there's been a lot of progress."

A 30-year-old Marvin Sordell can attest to that. As a young black player coming through the ranks around 2009 the lack of progress remained.

"People would say things like, 'Just keep your head down, you know, you'll hear things or things will be said or you'll get told to do things, just keep your head down.' And so you don't give them any excuse because they're looking for an excuse. That's difficult, and I don't know how much has changed because obviously I'm talking about being a young player. It's different when you're more established, but when you're a young player particularly, it can be very difficult, regardless of how talented you are. 'Maybe he has an attitude problem or there is this or that.' Straight away, it just makes things more difficult because you're fighting more barriers."

When Marcus Rashford, Jadon Sancho and Bukayo Saka received racial abuse on social media after the Euro 2020 final it was a yet another reminder that athletes who are not white often endure a level of hatred. The same is sadly also too often true for athletes who are not men, heterosexual or physically able. Eight years and countless examples earlier, Sordell was targeted by racial abuse on Twitter. Whether in the digital world or in the real one, athletes who are in some way not part of what much of society considers to be the conventional mould of a human being must not only live up to the unrealistic expectations of the sport they play but also face prejudice and discrimination that has nothing to do with their ability or performance.

"To be accepted you must be perfect," Sordell says. "Whereas for the other demographic it's just not the case, you can be accepted for who you are. It's amazing that Marcus Rashford has done incredible things, but it shouldn't have to take him doing incredible things for him to be accepted as an incredible football player. Look at Harry Kane, for example, he has had to deal with half of the things that Marcus has and yet he's lauded as such a hero around the country. I'm not saying he shouldn't be but the narrative is very different. It's because of that that he [Rashford] has to be perfect to be accepted... I think black people in the country would say you have to be exceptional to be good. My mom told me when I was very, very young, it's one of my earliest memories, that you have to work ten times harder, you have to be better. I had friends and I'd look at my friends and say: 'He's doing that, why can't I do that?' Because it won't ever be enough, and that really stuck with me."

That Sordell had to be better in all aspects of life just to have a chance at the same opportunities is a damning insight into the structural prejudice and discrimination that exists in the UK. That he did it in a high-performance sporting environment that continually pushes people to the limit is all the more impressive, but it didn't come without a cost.

The way Sordell talks about his career is hard to describe. Football was definitely a dream realised but it was also one that contained and confined him. Football as an industry stared him in the face and showed him what the priorities were, and they didn't include his well-being. "People were beyond second [in the priority list]... Get the result, bring the money in and then if you're right, great, and if not, figure it out," Sordell explains. The message was clear. You earn enough money, stick to your job, don't step out of your lane. There was no room for him to be who he wanted to be let alone room to figure out who that was.

"It [learning about himself] came from me suffering from depression, and really understanding at that point what the industry was," Sordell explains. "I didn't see them doing a lot of internal reflection to see who I was and what I wanted to be. From that period onwards, a lot of things changed in my career. I began to realise that this industry wasn't necessarily that suited to me. The environment of being a player wasn't necessarily suited to me. It was my dream to play and of course I was going to continue down that path but I figured I could be myself going through that period of time in my life. I did a lot of internal reflection and I became a lot more comfortable with who I am and that allowed me to then not have to take everything that happens within football as gospel. I began to think for myself a lot more and I began to change even more. I challenged even more when I thought things were wrong and just allowed myself to be me, and I knew that was going to be to the detriment of my career and I was comfortable with that."

And so he left the game. Chris Rush spoke earlier of the cost of football on his life and although in different situations and for different reasons both are examples of the extremes that football demands of the people involved in the sport.

Once his playing career was over though, Sordell's eyes were opened when he saw a dramatic change in appreciation for what he was saying now that he was no longer on the field.

"I guess I still have the platform I did when I was still playing, but when I speak now people come in and speak and agree with all the things I'm saying and take it in a positive way because I am just me, I'm not a football player. I'm just a producer, writer, public speaker, mental health advocate. People take it as that as opposed to just a football player speaking about stuff that you shouldn't really be speaking about. The reception is so, so different. It was almost overnight. I felt it. It was strange at first," Sordell admits, adding that there was even a bit of frustration at people agreeing with him when he called for more action in handling mental illness or dealing with racism because he had been saying it for years. "It's always the same thing, not wanting to listen to me because I should be concentrating on football, because I should know my role, but because I'm not a football player anymore, I'm positioned differently. I'm saying exactly the same thing in the same way. It's frustrating that I get praised for things now that previously I got a negative reception for."

In the past few years, the number of players speaking out about mental health has increased. Like any evolving, ongoing revolution, it seems some have to pay the price for a greater victory in the end.

"There have been quite a few moments in the past four or five years where people are starting to talk," Sordell says. "Danny Rose spoke very publicly and, as it is for a lot of players, some people take the hit. I took the hit. Danny Rose took a hit. He was praised, rightly so, but some fall by the wayside and have to kind of go away and rebuild."

Their bravery and the bravery of many others created a strong foundation for changing modern perception around mental health and as a result the idea of the athlete as a person. The pandemic was also a big catalyst for change as mental health became something many more people had to confront. It was a huge moment in public understanding but also in the way in which athletes were viewed. Social media gave athletes greater power to connect and share, but it also gave them the chance to show their support and talk, unfiltered, about how they felt. It's a medium full of problems, but one that also possesses great power.

"We understand now we have more of the power and we can be the ones who play this game," Sordell says. "If we want to stop this game, we can stop this game... Players are beginning to understand their true value within this industry."

Sordell is no longer a player but he has certainly recognised his power. As a producer at ONEIGHTY he tells stories about players' lives that feel real. He has a theory that one of the main ways players are dehumanised is through the constant use of their surnames. The idea that we are further away from someone by calling them by a less personal name, aka their family name, is intriguing and indeed when considered there is a clear difference between the thought process when hearing, for example, Raheem rather than Sterling.

Two years ago, Sordell went to the PFA (Professional Footballers' Association) and explained his idea about having someone at clubs but directly attached to them to help with player well-being. His idea was met with interest and he was told "plans were in place" but such things "take time" and so "patience was required". While the role of Player Care has taken on and continues to take on greater importance in terms of human development at clubs, a designated person in place for the well-being of athletes is still a work in progress for many sports teams around the world, let alone football teams in England. The NRL teams in Australia have created a system that works for them in which there are many valuable lessons others can learn from but any decision made towards putting Sordell's idea or other similar ideas into practice must consider the context of the league and the motivation for such a role being implemented.

Ultimately what Sordell and many others are after is not something complicated, but a basic level of care. "It's not a ridiculous thing to suggest that every single person in a leadership role in any entity should have some empathy for and take care of their employees," Sordell argues, poignantly. "I'm talking about basic levels of empathy and treating you like you matter and that you're not just there to fill space, and not just because you play football. You're a human being first before you're a football player. Managers must understand how to manage people first, players second, and know how to get the best out of them. The financial crisis aside, I think a lot of the time clubs find it difficult, I guess particularly given the growing market and how finances have changed so much. Because players get paid so much more, they feel like they need to squeeze every ounce out of them. It's using it as an excuse: because they're paid more money you can treat them how you want."

It's clear that football didn't look after Sordell the person and that it took enormous levels of work on his part to get to where he is today. That he is using his current platform to create honest stories as well as campaign for the well-being of others speaks to his character.

Ramsey is trying to implement human development the best way he can in a system that is designed to make that harder for him and the kids he works with. But his desire to learn more about both his work and the work of others reveals someone who believes life is one enormous ecosystem and that to serve each part independently is to be less effective. He knows how much is at play and how winning changes narratives but not the truth of a situation. "One swing of the leg validates so much in football," Ramsey says. Such narratives can lead to more unrealistic expectations, inaccurate assessment and misjudgment of holistic factors. The score never tells the whole story.

There is much more to the pair's story than in these pages but their shared feeling across two wildly different eras of football that the game only cared for Ramsey and Sordell and not for Chris and Marvin is a poignant reminder that for all of the change happening now in human development it has been far too long in arriving. Whatever the context of any time, people should be treated with respect and given the chance to grow beyond their profession. In the nearly 30 years between the two careers, that lesson has still not been learned. Black and ethnic minority coaches are still competing in a game rigged against them and the identity of footballers is still being reduced to just performance. As Chris Ramsey said: "It's a long time for a little progress."

13

Soul

The word soul is tied to a raft of religious, philosophical and musical meanings. It can casually refer to what type of person someone is, e.g. "He's an old soul" or be connected to soul music, a genre characterised by the intensity of feeling in rhythm and blues. Either way, the word has always been linked to character, to an inner music of some sort. In Old English soul was sawol, defined as a "spiritual and emotional part of a person." It is the essence of ourselves and perhaps what remains once the flesh fades. Whatever you believe, the soul is who we really are.

In sport, there doesn't seem to be much room for that. Athletes, and often coaches, have to find ways to win and perform even if that means removing or hiding who they really are. Looking at the big picture in sport, one where athletes' bodies are being asked to endure more for longer and under even greater pressure, it's hard to believe that sport cares at all about anything beyond the result and the profit. Perhaps its greatest luxury is that it knows it will always have a steady supply of people willing to sacrifice more than they should to be in that jersey, on that field.

In all the people I spoke to for *Soul*, I found there are people making a difference, people who have opted to recognise the importance of the person. There are undoubtedly thousands of others but they are still rare. All are still fighting against structures that value performance, profit and results over anything else. Competition is great and it's one of the main reasons people love sport, but if that is all that matters then there's a problem.

Perhaps, like most things in life, the greatest question is around balance. Ultimately the main question of *Soul* is: can you play sport at a high level and still look after, nurture who you are as a person? Given the number of people who play professional sport around the world the answer to that is probably yes, but there's also no denying that for many people sport has cost them an awful lot when it comes to their humanity.

Athletes experience joy, feel love, suffer sorrow and loss the same as those who watch them. Those emotions are tied to the greatest moments in our lives. Some may argue they are what makes a life, but do athletes feel they can show these emotions, and if not why not? What happens if you work in an environment that doesn't allow for you to investigate other parts of your personality, to ask deeper questions about who you are and what you want to be, to give you room to be present rather than constantly having to think about the next game? Who do you become if winning isn't enough, if the moment you become successful attempts are made to find something negative about you or to instantly focus on the next possible achievement?

The answers are complex and unclear, and are certainly not all to be found in *Soul*. Undoubtedly though, there is no one answer. There is no one approach that works for all, but beyond the importance of working within your own context was recognising that the way in which professional sport has developed over the last few years is intrinsically connected to the way in which western society has focussed on unprecedented and largely unregulated growth. The quest for more has trickled down into the everyday aspects of professional sport. Anything is rarely enough in the modern era. There are always more records, more games, more accolades, more achievements. But beyond dedication to improvement of skills or fitness, which is a natural and necessary part of a life in professional sport, lies an area of potential one-dimensionality.

But athletes are not - cannot be - one-dimensional. They are people too. Who they are off the field, court and track not only affects their performance but is an important part of their life. While the outside world may only remember an athlete for their professional achievements or a headline here or there, that athlete's life extends beyond the lines on the court. There is more than just the number of games played, trophies collected or social media followers.

What is a life made up of? For an athlete it may appear that scoring the winner in a cup final or being the fastest in your competition is the peak of a life's achievements. It is in fact the peak of the athlete's professional achievements. This may also rank as a great moment in their life, but the people they share their life with, the moments of emotion that everyone can relate to, those are the peak of life's achievements. Are they moments that must be shared with the public? Absolutely not, but they are moments that the public must remember when watching the athlete.

Inside sport, when athletes grow in an environment where the focus on sport is too great, where sport becomes the determining factor for existence, then both the athletes and the environment are one-dimensional. Our existence, athlete or not, is much more than what we do. I believe it all starts with where we are.

Walking in the woods, swimming in the sea and running on the sand - these are valuable moments of connection with the natural world. For the most part they are moments we often take for granted, but there is a regenerative force to be felt amongst the natural world, the place that has made all life possible. It is also a reminder that while development at all costs can lead to great success in one field, the resulting impact on other areas of life can be terrible. In turn, we have to ask what that impact does to our success.

Much like the earth needs enough trees to survive, so people need others in our lives to make it a life. Those people act like trees, removing the dangerous air to increase the growth, diversity and understanding of our own biosphere.

History shows that back when wealth and possessions were not the ultimate goal, human nature was originally about harmonious relationships with each other and the surrounding world. Clearly the world is different now and money can bring opportunity and stability, but it shouldn't be the driving force. It shouldn't make us forget the importance of the people and the environment around us.

Indeed, even the way the natural world is being destroyed reflects what is happening between humans. Managing that ecosystem rather than just crops, which are the end product, is to have an awareness of the whole. This is no different to people in systems around the world. Focussing only on their output, what they produce, is to miss the multitude of impacts the surrounding environment has on them. A crop is affected by the soil, the air, the climate to name but a few factors. The same is true of a human life.

NM Gwynne writes in *Gwynne's Grammar*: "*Without words we can feel but we cannot think... If we are to think correctly and usefully, words need to be used correctly... using words correctly involves two sciences. One of them is vocabulary, the science of what words mean. The other is grammar, the science of how words are used... Vocabulary and grammar are therefore sciences which are the necessary prelude to the science of thinking.*"

Once breathing and in the world, words are at the heart of all that we do. What we say, how we say it and all the non-verbal language that accompanies words, is the basis of our existence. We must use the right language because if we do not understand the words we use to describe what we are doing how can we possibly expect to end up where we want to be?

A lot of the language around human development is often scientific, with difficult words and long sentences with a number of clauses. There is great value in a lot of the research and academic work done in these areas, but too often this work occurs in an academic bubble. By the nature of its structure and language used, it often remains inaccessible to many. If we want some of these ideas to become more widespread and available to more people, then we must make it easier to understand and more accessible. At the same time, we must also make sure that easier to understand ideas are still founded in solid evidence and experiences. If we are to bridge the gap between the worlds of academia and accessible learning then we must keep our balance. In short, the words we choose to say to one another matter, but so do their origins.

Given that it doesn't seem too inaccurate to suggest that too much of the language in any high-pressure environment but especially football is not restorative, this approach is appropriate. The pandemic has forced us to consider a great deal about our lives, perhaps nothing more than the fragility of it. We are a vulnerable people, whether we care to admit it or not.

That vulnerability is connected to a desire to figure out who we are, and once that is found, finding our place in the world. This is our personality but also our character, a word defined as "the mental and ethical traits individualising a person, group, or nation." The word character hails from the Greek *kharaktēr*, which means "imprint on the soul." Our soul is the essence of who we are. If sport doesn't care about that, then it's exploiting bodies and minds for profit and victories.

Liverpool's academy director, Alex Inglethorpe, told *The Coaches' Voice* about character in an interview:

"Talent can get you to 16, but I believe it's character that gets you to 35. I think you can play youth team football when you're talented. But if you want to play to 35, then it's about resilience, ability to withstand pressure, ability to evaluate a bit more honestly... Everything rests on character. Character is what defines you when you leave your youth team days behind and enter the senior world."

Intriguingly, Inglethorpe believes it is getting harder and harder for coaches in all industries to find out whether a player has character or not. Following the etymology of the word, it's clear that everyone has character. This is not a question of what is right or wrong though, but rather how to provide the opportunity for people to develop their character in a way that fits in with the values of the team, club, company or family.

Player care roles are changing things. As Hugo Scheckter outlined in this book the need for and the value of personal development roles is increasing. At Manchester United, Dr Chris McCready is doing some fascinating work with identity and personal development at the club and recently published a PhD explicitly outlining that it was possible to help nurture an identity beyond the idea of just being a footballer.

"Multiple players interpreted their club environments as encouraging them to view themselves as footballers constantly, and become a 24hr (24/7) footballer... Indeed, empirical data suggested that the 24/7 approach was not seen as conducive to performance."

Football clubs are recognising the changing and diverse landscape of human development, and the need to keep up. This change is long overdue.

Tottenham Hotspur advertised in August 2021 for a mental health and emotional well-being manager, a virtually unseen position in England but an encouraging sign of the aforementioned change in action. Perhaps one of the reasons the various roles connected to human development remain rare in England is because of strategies like the Elite Player Performance Plan (EPPP) or organisations like the LFE (League Football Education).

In the Premier League, the EPPP has been in place since 2012. This strategy is designed to create more homegrown players through a player-led approach. There are four pillars, one of which is education, and the EPPP statement includes the following:

"The Premier League aims to provide world-class education via inspirational and innovative teaching, which develops educationally rounded people through the delivery of a holistic approach... to support the technical, tactical, physical, mental, lifestyle and welfare development of all Academy players."

How clubs deliver this holistic approach is largely up to them, but digging a little deeper leaves some questions unanswered. Education remains a cornerstone of development, but does the personal development of a person need to be connected to education? Ideally all areas are connected, but given that personal development is the foundation for so many other areas it seems odd to have it included in a section that is perhaps most likely linked to finishing off school qualifications or providing employment opportunities should a career in football not be an option. As Chris Ramsey pointed out, both are required and valuable but there is more to human development than a subsection in education.

Given that in the Premier League handbook player care is defined as "the adoption of a holistic approach to personal and sporting development, supporting Academy players to achieve their potential in and out of football" it seems perhaps fair to suggest that personal development is less a feature in education and much more a part of player care. If that is the case, and it is worth noting that not every academy is the same, then it is intriguing that in the handbook player care appears to only be mentioned in connection with academy work. Granted, player care in a first team is very different to that of an academy as Scheckter mentioned in chapter six, but this implies that personal development is some sort of workshop rather than a continuous act that the right club philosophy can have an enormous impact on.

If we give the wording the benefit of the doubt and assume that education is being used in the broader sense of learning, then sadly issues remain based on the rankings of academies. In England, academy ratings rank from a category 1 (the best) to a category 4. Intriguingly though, only a category 1 and 2 academy needs to employ someone full time in player care. Academies rated category 3 or 4 "may nominate an existing member of academy staff" to do that job. This is jarring for many reasons.

Firstly, that member of staff likely already has enough "other jobs" that they are trying to do alongside their primary work (and is likely not financially compensated for it). Secondly, what kind of message does that send? Only if your academy is elite do we think it is worth then also considering the person's well-being. Worse still, it is those leading academies that then get more funding. Of course there will be individuals in category 3 and 4 academies who care for people, but they are without proper support, framework or compensation with which to make personal development something long-lasting and perhaps even club wide.

Even more damning is the excellent research presented in Nicola A. Sothern and Jimmy O'Gorman's paper published in *Soccer & Society* called "Exploring the mental health and well-being of professional academy footballers in England." Inside they state that: "*Closer examination of and support for the mental health and well-being of junior elite footballers contracted to development programmes must be considered by stakeholders in football academies and policy makers in football authorities.*"

While the data they reveal is small, it is also disheartening to read about how 14-year-olds are struggling to make strong social connections, how important mental toughness was and how they avoided talking about thoughts or feelings that may be considered 'weak'. Again, while an isolated incident, the revelation from one 13-year-old player about the EPPP's supposed support network made for grim reading:

"*However, P9 along with seven other participants were unaware of who their designated welfare officers were and communicated never having contact with them. In addition, advice given to professional academy footballers often reinforced stigma in relation to challenges to mental health. Two participants revealed that they had intermittent contact with a sports psychologist in the form of attending workshops. The information the participants received tended to encourage the concealment or self-management of emotions, strategies designed to enhance performance.*"

Beyond academies, there are also questions about human development in the first team. When players reach the top of the club the need for personal development becomes much harder, again as Scheckter illuminated in chapter six. Nonetheless, the difficulty remains striking given that for many this is also a time of transition, with huge shifts in expectation, possibility and means. Why does making it into the first team warrant the lack of support that might have been on offer during young years? Human development is not a phase like puberty. It is always ongoing.

In his book *Emotional Intelligence: Why it can matter more than IQ, Daniel Goleman states that "even though a high IQ is no guarantee of prosperity, prestige or happiness in life, our schools and our culture fixate on academic abilities, ignoring emotional intelligence, a set of traits - some might call it character - that also matters immensely for our personal destiny."*

A cultural fixation over numbers, grades or statistics is a major problem. The reduction of a person to a number or value is dehumanising and hardly gives any real insight into the individual's capabilities. The person is not completely disregarded in player assessment of course, but analytics are a new religion. They too are important and should not be ignored, but just like praying to God for something to happen is to miss the point of faith, so is expecting numbers to tell you the whole story.

Furthermore, how much of that human assessment is limited to the recruitment stage? When a player signs for a new club, their ability to handle emotion, apply critical thinking or understand their character traits requires regular attention, and must be considered beyond just whether or not a player would make a good signing. Sadly, as previous coaches have explained, battles against pre-existing structures, the obsession over finding the next generational talent or pressure to deliver results so as to keep the business moving in the right direction, have often seen the human aspect become an afterthought.

Without the integration of human development across a club, the best possible chance of success will remain beyond reach. The entire process of human development should always match the club's philosophy, culture and structure. A "plug in and play" approach to human development will not, cannot work.

Also important to note is that however human development is introduced at a club, it should always be done in connection with personal development leaders and sports psychologists. The idea of developing someone's character is to supplement the work of those already working in the personal development areas, hopefully providing athletes with the opportunity to find a far greater understanding of themselves and their emotions. The skin is being strengthened first rather than having to apply a bandage to it later on.

How often are athletes given space to talk about how they feel? For too long interpretations of masculinity perpetuated the idea that men were not supposed to show emotion. For too long women have wrongfully had to fight against the idea that they're always overflowing with emotion. This is about taking a look at ourselves, having those perhaps difficult conversations and making an active decision to improve our ability to understand the emotions that make us humans.

In the aforementioned book *The Open Door*, Helen Keller

outlines her musings on life and faith. The book, written in 1957, by Keller, who was deaf and blind, strikes a cord that few writers ever achieve. *The American Foundation for the Blind* has an entire archive for Keller, including some of the book review clippings from the late 1950s. All of them rave about Keller's philosophical thoughts and how groundbreaking they are and will continue to be in the years ahead. On character, Keller says the following:

"Character cannot be developed in ease and quiet. Only through experience of trial and suffering can the soul be strengthened, vision cleared, ambition inspired, and success achieved."

Keller is right. The best place for a person to grow is through experience, although it need not always be a trial of suffering. In Twelfth Night Shakespeare wrote: "If music be the food of love, play on." Indeed, if words are the food of the soul then we must speak on, if only to understand how important accuracy of language is.

Perhaps one way to enhance character development through use of language is to create a list of all of the character traits that a person has with the person in question, then discuss the traits they want to develop and the ones that the organisation believes is integral to those who represent it. Once this list has been established, then it is time to break each one down into what, who and how, i.e. what is the trait, who are the people in your life that this trait applies to and how can we develop it, perhaps through activities or conversation with the people we think embody the trait.

Take commitment as a character trait that one person might want to develop. The first step is to establish what it means. Commitment is defined as: bound to a person or thing, as by pledge or assurance; devoted. Once this is understood on terms the individual can recognise then examples of that can be discussed. Some might say their partners are committed to them through marriage or love or devotion to helping them pursue their goals in professional sport. Others might say, their head coach or teammates. Using that relatable and relevant information can help spark discussion around how to show more commitment, and this is of course where Keller's quote comes into play.

Being out in the world, with people and experiencing different activities, is the best way to gain a better understanding of a trait. It is of course possible and important for people to want to show their partners that they too are committed if they feel that is lacking, or to show their head coach how committed they are - and the best ways to do that can be discussed, such as spending some time not focussing on your sport but on what is important to your partner, or, in the case of showing the head coach, doing extra training sessions or going out of your way to make sure your teammates are doing well. But it is more likely that spending time in a new environment with new people is likely to raise questions and emotions that can help to grow the understanding of the desired trait more organically. The best example of this would be for athletes to spend time in the communities that they serve, from those leading the community to those struggling to survive in it. Many sports organisations across the world already do this, but there is a need to do this without the cameras or the social media posts, which whether we like it or not play a role in how we act, but rather just for the experience itself. The world of live recording is hard to truly escape for many professional athletes and clubs, but it is possible to make sure that the experience of understanding a community leads not only to a greater sense of pride but also to a greater sense of character development.

The list of character traits is long, perhaps even endless and each time the answer might be different but the key is that the process is clear and relatable for the person in question. Understand what it is you want to develop, who in your life does it and how you want to go about exemplifying that trait are three steps towards developing the character of young athletes today.

In the modern era the way the pursuit of a career has been sold as the ultimate has not only led to a disconnection from people's own understanding of themselves, but also the community they represent. When speaking with her husband, former US President Barack Obama, the former First Lady, Michelle Obama, said on her *The Michelle Obama Podcast*:

"I came to learn the same thing you learned. While working on the 47th floor of a fancy law firm and making all that money, that it felt lonely and isolating. I had this amazing view of the south-east side of the city from my office, I could see the lake and all of the neighbourhood that I had come from and I never felt further from that neighbourhood than when I was sitting in that

office, working on briefs and cases that had nothing to do with anything that helped a broader group of people outside of myself. And it felt lonely."

If athletes are lonely then sport has failed them. Admittedly, this isn't made any easier by overloading of information and life updates that are designed to make most feel inadequate. In their book *Factfulness*, Hans Rosling and his son Ola Rosling and daughter-in-law Anna Rosling Rönnlund believe this overloading is why humans don't really see reality for what it is. As a result of this self-implemented filter though, we are more likely to care about dramatic events and therefore end up with an inaccurate perspective of the world. Factfulness, a word the authors created, is a skill that allows you to recognise the types of stories that get attention because of the dramatic triggers they have. In the book, the Rosling's state: *"Factfulness is recognising that a single perspective can limit your imagination, and remembering that is better to look at a problem from many angles to get a more accurate understanding and find practical solutions."*

One of the most obvious representations of this is on social media, but given that there are over 50,000 results on Amazon when you search their books section for the word 'leadership' it is clear that the same is also true for buzzwords of the modern era. We currently live in age of overloading leadership experts as many people from different parts of the world with contrasting experiences and understandings of it share their thoughts. Any opportunity to improve understanding is welcomed, or at least should be, but this leaves most of us overwhelmed in our attempts at understanding what it is to lead let alone how to put it into practice. And herein lies the key. There are, evidently, tens of thousands of books on how to be the best leader but how many truly excellent leaders do you know? The same is true for books about empathy or compassion or mindfulness. It is one thing to write about it, another to read about it and an entirely different thing to put practices into the appropriate action for yourself, your team or community.

In 2001, Jim Collins explained the concept of leadership levels in an article in the *Harvard Business Review*. Collins later listed level 5, the top level, as one of the seven characteristics of great companies in a book called *From Good to Great*. His interpretation is clean, uses simple language and works extremely well when assessing leadership in a sporting context.

Intriguingly, following Collins' definitions, the word 'leader' does not even appear until the final two levels of the model. Perhaps this is proof that too often the word is misused and that when someone shows signs of commitment or competence that is not to be confused with leading, a trait that requires a combination of many other traits in order to be genuine.

The long and short of it is I think we need to spend more time looking after one another. Whether it's because of a lack of time or because pre-existing methodology forces individuals to be viewed through specific categories that no longer truly reflect who a person really is, there is often a neglect of the individual. And in a sport like football, a lack of money is quite frankly not a valid excuse. The harder truth is more likely that the focus on the person is not often enough a priority.

In a 2021 interview with *Wisden Cricket Monthly*, former England spinner and head coach of Sussex County Cricket Club, Ian Salisbury, spoke about the importance of considering the person before anything else, how in contrast that was to previous years in professional cricket where vulnerability was seen as a weakness.

"I think it's an insult to think you can coach a team or a bunch of individuals without any knowledge of them. How can you ask them to do something without knowing anything about them? So just show that you care for them. Show a bit of empathy, it just helps. They don't remember you teaching them how to bowl that ball or hit that shot. Do you help them in life to become a better person? That's the job."

Indeed, in Barney Douglas' 2019 documentary *The Edge* about the reinvention of English cricket the blunt truth about pursuing the number one ranking is exposed in moving and brilliant fashion. Former England wicketkeeper Matt Prior succinctly explains the cost of pursuing excellence: "Life as a professional sportsman doesn't necessarily lend itself to you being a good person – because it's about winning."

Jonathan Trott, one of Prior's teammates and one of England's batsmen, has spoken about his mental health struggles through that time and is in tears at one point during the documentary. That England team achieved their goal and will undoubtedly be remembered as one of the greatest test cricket teams in the world, but the scars of that victory are evident.

For groups to have a better understanding of one another they have to spend time together in settings not limited to the sport they play. After all, the development of character occurs through experience, as Keller wrote. That involves the person in question spending time with others, being in their or other communities, learning and interacting with new people, experiencing something that gets them feeling. In that sense, they are never alone.

In his now legendary piece in *Esquire* magazine, Tom Junod writes the following about the former children's television presenter, Mr Rogers:

"Fred Rogers didn't want to go to heaven, he wanted to live in heaven, here, now, in this world, and so one day, when he was talking about all the people he had loved in his life, he looked at me and said, 'The connections we make in the course of a life - maybe that's what heaven is, Tom. We make so many connections here on earth. Look at us - I've just met you, but I'm investigating in who you are and who you will be, and I can't help it.'"

Being alive is magical, but like anything in life its value becomes so much greater when we share it with others. In a group that has consciously decided to develop more than just professional ability, I believe this work can have a profound impact.

Soul is not designed to provide a definitive answer to the problem of how to apply a greater focus on the person rather than the player in football. I was fortunate to learn a great deal from all the teams I visited and the coaches I spoke to, and their approaches are unique and cannot simply be copy and pasted into another setting. What I want achieve with *Soul* is just to show that it is possible.

There are no shortcuts. It requires work to develop yourself or help others. To think otherwise is to fall into the classic trap of trying to apply a simple approach to a complex system. It is not easy to avoid being lulled into this approach. Take the burgeoning self-help industry, for example. While it is helpful that there are now more resources available to people looking to try and understand themselves better or to look at changing their own approach, perhaps we should be thinking about why it is a burgeoning industry.

Not only is it more difficult to decide what to do to help oneself, but it is also difficult to decipher what is real, what is for show and what is personal experience made public for the wrong reasons. It feels like too often perception has overtaken actual ability or value. Popular science in the hands of those without a deep understanding of the science is dangerous.

Beyond the understanding of the ideas we are presenting comes the question of what happened to letting the work or the experience stand for itself? Of course we must operate and move within new digital spaces in order to be relevant in our fields, but why does everything have to be marketed and sold? The competition that breeds is harmful and often forces out space for more empathy, which is all the more ironic if the work about self-help is guided towards more human development.

After all, let us consider how many of those feeling the need to turn to self-help books might be doing so because they have been made, by the forces of the world around them, to feel inadequate in the first place? Are we asking ourselves whether that is right or are we too concerned by looking to offer solutions to apparent problems? I can't help but feel that too often we are transmitting a perspective that life-changing answers lie at the end of 300 pages. Not only are we selling shortcuts when there are none, but we are missing the point that life-changing answers come in different shapes, sizes and moments. They are extremely personal to each person, and will be different for each person. That is what makes each of our lives unique.

Different areas will resonate for different people. Not everything you read, hear or see will strike a chord and perhaps inspire you to take that knowledge and actively put it into practice. Each person has experienced growth, relationships, emotions, stress, work and health differently, and so it is only natural that each person's response to help varies. That is why one definitive answer or approach cannot work. And that is perhaps the hardest truth for us all.

Dennis Hörtin at AIK said: "Don't look at a template or a blueprint or a curriculum, focus your attention on what's actually going on. Pay attention, get deep insights and from there you can make informed decisions in the moment that are probably likely to be more suited for that context as opposed to a theory or a curriculum that someone would like to adopt."

Thinking on your feet, acknowledging the environment around you and making informed decisions on the basis of that interaction rather than because of a suggested model is an important step towards better human development. I have learned so much while writing *Soul* that there is no definitive lesson. Indeed, as aforementioned, there is no one way to make human development work for everyone. There were five considerations though, that I couldn't get away from. Naturally they would be realised differently across the world but their premise was true and so they felt worthy of highlighting.

Values first, business later

Firstly, that everyone at the club agrees to a values-based approach rather than an economic one. It's the impossible promise in modern sport but it's the one worth making if organisations truly want to stand for something greater than profit margins, wins and jerseys sold. If clubs are focussed on holistic principles as the aim and not numerical ones then more human development is likely to follow.

What is it that people value in their life? What is it that drives them, that gives them reason to get up every morning? For many people this will be the people in their life, their family and friends. For many it may also be the drive to make a change or to help others or to change the world. Whatever it is, it must be understood by all involved in the development of the person in question.

Success is the most recurring drive for athletes. Players play the game to win, but how is that success achieved and is it therefore the only form of success worth measuring yourself by? The tangible success of holding a trophy is not linear. You do not do X enough times and get Y. By illuminating myriad factors that contribute to success it becomes clearer that success is not a result of doing one or two things, or a direct result of one action, bur rather a culmination of factors interacting with one another. Those factors are often connected to relationships with others, such as family and friends. Not only can the existence and maintenance of those relationships then be seen as successful in their own right, they also illuminate the context of success because without them, winning a trophy would not have been possible.

Imagine a team that all wanted to be successful, but was aware of the true depth of that statement. That sporting success might mean something different to others and that for all of them it was not linear; that recognition of success off the playing field was necessary for stronger mental health, greater collective understanding and on-field success; and that the culmination of all of this could make an enormous difference to achieving a goal.

For any value to be protected, challenges must be embraced, preparation for adversity must be in place and the victories along the way must be enjoyed and not just considered stepping stones towards the ultimate goal. Once the understanding of their values exists, then it's important to discuss what might threaten that along the way. In the case of success, that could be a number of things from injury, team form, mental health or a different head coach. Understanding how to deal with those challenges when they come - because they will - will help make the burden of them easier to bear when they do. "*When one door of happiness closes, another opens; but often we look so long at the closed door that we do not see the one which has been opened for us,*" the remarkable author and activist Helen Keller poignantly wrote in her book *The Open Door*. These words ring true for life in sport as well. The constant drive to achieve and the failure that accompanies that pursuit leaves many looking longingly at the door now closed. With more guidance, this does not need to be the case. It is possible to help people not only see the open door, but to step through it.

If the club believes in nurturing values then the onus will be on conversation, relationships, openness and a bond built around what represents the club. It is time for clubs to really think about what sets them apart, rather than falling back on the familiar values that line dressing rooms and gyms around the world. In elite sport, everyone is trying to be ruthless, to have an edge and to be fearless, but are those the values that best represent your players and your team? In the age where big clubs and teams in sport dominate headlines, interests and often the field of play, there are still ways to build an identity.

Coach and writer Alex Clapham revealed insights into the academy at Athletic Bilbao in an article originally posted on *Cano Football*. In it, the club's then sporting director José Amorrortu explains his belief in values, how the children have lots of responsibilities such as sorting the kit or carrying equipment, and how many of the older teenagers are doing degrees at universities. Amorrortu is quoted as saying: "nobody has what we have. We have a culture here, an identity. It's our job to create good people as well as good players, and nobody does that like we do."

While it is encouraging to hear Amorrortu speak so passionately about creating good people as well as good players, it is wrong to say that no other club has a culture or an identity. Every club in the world has that. The question is whether they are harnessing it in the same, positive way that Bilbao evidently are. The Spanish club runs festivals for book publishing, literature and film, and as Sid Lowe wrote in *The Guardian* such events are an important way of the club showing who they are at a time when it is perhaps harder than ever to win trophies: *"There must be something other than success, some other measurement of it... There must be something, full stop. So there is: themselves. Yet it goes beyond that, to something more universal, to ideals celebrated in others too."* In sharing our identity, we can build a bond with others built on what we believe in rather than what we achieve.

Adopt and adapt, don't plug in and play

It is pivotal that while the essence of different approaches to human development can be adopted, and in many cases should be, they must always be done within the context of your own environment. Failure to do so is to expect such a model to follow a plug in and play function that rarely works in most cases but especially not in the case of developing human beings. However clubs want to improve their human development, their culture must mesh with the desired methodology to stand a greater chance of a positive outcome in developing human beings.

Taking AIK, Bilbao or Nordsjælland's approach and plugging it into your own would be nothing short of a lazy attempt to solve a complex problem. In doing so, there's a total disregard for the coaching culture and indeed many other non-football aspects of culture that have an impact on the way the sport is played in the country and the way people coach and communicate. While not a football team, the team working at the Fuyao factory shown in the Netflix documentary *American Factory* also struggled with having Chinese methods and expectations of work inserted into an American factory. If a team wins a tournament that should not instantly mean that the factors that led to that victory could also be applied to your own potential victory. By all means, assess the success and the factors that led to it but recognise that your culture, approach and system is different and that that needs to be taken into consideration when planning for what you want to achieve. Again, that doesn't mean be afraid of change, but it does mean recognise what makes you unique.

A process for all

Those involved in delivering human development, in whatever form, also need to be included and not just considered a part of the equation. They cannot always be leaned on without having some level of support and room to grow themselves. If that ends up being the case then we are simply adding room for human development to one area whilst simultaneously removing it from another. Of course, the young children in an academy and players in general are the focus subject in terms of human development because they are the ones traversing the rocky world of the playing world. However, youth is not a prerequisite for human development. We are always capable of learning, and our coaching staff needs not only to have support around them but also be helped in their own attempts to develop emotional understanding and grow areas of their character. Fergus Connolly, a performance expert who has worked with some of the biggest teams in sport, put it perfectly: "Sometimes even the sheepdog needs a sheepdog."

Be wary of endless development

Just because the player is in the first team or has reached high levels of performance does not mean personal development is over or no longer necessary. While it is always possible to get better in sport there is danger that comes with that. The sacrifice of contentment and appreciation for a literal never-ending drive towards performance excellence is a problem. Furthermore it also limits appreciation for non-sporting growth. Life is so big and broad even the use of the word 'results' sees growth in that space considered incomprehensible, whereas sport has the tangible advantage of boundaries, rules and numbers to offer as evidence. This work matters in academies and in first teams. It matters in all sports and all areas of professional work. Physical health and professional ability cannot be the only means of measuring development, and some teams around the world have recognised this. We are all running on different circuits at different speeds. This is not, unlike almost every other aspect of sport, a competition. This is about understanding how to manage your own life, outside of the race you run to compete every weekend.

Language, language, language

Whether to guide conversation through Motivational

Interviewing, use more restorative language in day-to-day exchanges, or adapt and find the appropriate way to speak despite cultural differences, language matters.

Words are what we use to define our actions, feelings and the world. If we are not clear about what we mean then we cannot expect to have clear outcomes. If we are not clear about what someone else is saying then we cannot expect to know them.

Furthermore, there is much to be gained looking beyond the comfort of the English language. Other languages have different flows and while learning the native language will help you connect with people it will also open another world of understanding about how your own language works.

For any of these approaches to be considered, clubs first have to make a conscious decision to believe in human development. Dr Chris McCready's aforementioned research into the troubles of the 24/7 footballer prove that work is being done to change this belief. That is necessary because one-dimensionality suits no one. Clubs cannot afford to see personal development as an extra. Clubs who can't afford this approach need support to do so, and those who can need to understand the real value in doing so rather than just doing it to tick a box. The pressure to deliver results or make financial profits cannot come into consideration in this regard. If we do not consider human development a priority in football, then not only is that reductionist and exploitative it is also a damning reflection of the sport's landscape today.

In a 2020 paper written in the *Sport, Education and Society journal* by Noora J. Ronkainen, Kenneth Aggerholm, Tatiana V. Ryba & Jacquelyn Allen-Collinson, the topic of life skills to existential learning is explored and what is clear is that *"we should not assume that developing and transferring skills is easy; that we are far from understanding the transfer process, and some scholars challenge whether it exists at all; and that there is cultural variation in what skills are recognised as such or valued in workplaces or life in general."*

We are very much at the beginning of our understanding about human development in sport, but the last sentence in this quote from the journal reminds us just how big the hurdle of recognition is. We must all take steps to realise that developing human beings is necessary. However we do it, we must do it. Otherwise, we will continue to reduce human beings to commodities and numbers. And human lives end, numbers don't.

Legendary Schalke youth coach Norbert Elgert, who trained the likes of Mesut Özil and Leroy Sane, knows a lot about numbers. The numbers of great players he has trained, the numerous teams he has coached, the thousands of players he has helped. Echoing the sentiment of Liverpool's academy director Alex Inglethorpe, Elgert talked about character development on the excellent *Rasenfunk* podcast: *"Talent puts you on the doorstep, but attitude, character, perseverance are what get you through the door. You need talent to make the most of your talent. You need a talent to deal with obstacles and opposition."*

That is what human development really is about - helping people get through the door of both their professional career and their lives during and beyond sport. This of course extends to coaches as well. Elgert believes that empathy and emotional intelligence are pivotal for a coach to be successful. The need to return to the German word *Menschenfänger*, a regular and favourite word in *Mensch*, arises once more. That is what is at the heart of good coaching. You need to catch people with your enthusiasm, so much so that they will follow you. Part of the way to do that is not just helping them become better players, but also people with a greater understanding of themselves.

DeForest Buckner, an NFL defensive tackle, told *NBC Sports'* Jennifer Lee Chan the following about Robert Saleh, his former Defensive Coordinator at the San Fransisco 49ers and who was appointed the head coach of the New York Jets early 2021.

"With Saleh, it's not just about football and the X's and O's," Buckner said, referring to the tactical approach of American football. "He wants to teach you about life and build a relationship to get to know you personally. Which is why it was so easy to play for him... Yes, he is a phenomenal coach who will make the right adjustments throughout a game and always put you in position to succeed, but it's his ability to connect with you and have you fired up and ready to play, week in and week out, no matter the circumstances."

If there ever was a clear piece of evidence that connecting with the person before the player was the most effective way to coach then here it is. Buckner explicitly outlines that it is easier to do his job - and notably, given Buckner's performances under Saleh and since, to a high standard as well - when you knew the man coaching you was helping you learn about life as much as the weekend's game plan.

It seems fair to say that someone who has a greater understanding of themselves and their emotions is in a better place. If we are willing to do the work then we can understand ourselves better and are more likely to develop our character. We are more likely to be self-aware of our own emotions, confront fear and use emotions wisely in social contexts. Ultimately, to realise that we are not better without emotions, that emotions are a huge part of what makes us human beings and that to have an understanding of them stands us in better stead for life. If we can do this then we stand a greater chance of succeeding, however we define that success. In this context, the only comparative use of 'better' is yourself before doing the work on growing your character.

Even then the word 'better' should be given some distance, because ultimately it is up to you to decide if you are doing better. We are constantly being told and sold ways to be and do better, and yet are given no time to consider whether that is really the better we want or need. In his timely book *Notes on a Nervous Planet*, Matt Haig rightly points out that often in the world today many people suffer from the idea that *"we could be better than who we are if we tried to become something else."* The idea behind human development is not to become something else, but rather to be a happier, stronger, clearer, more confident version of yourself. This is about understanding what you care about, understanding how to keep your mind sharp and your emotions smart, your empathy high even in the face of competition, and how to keep the world healthy through your own choices. This is not a ten-step plan to change your life, or a list of products that you need in order to be 'more beautiful' inside and out. Character development does not happen through enforcing change upon a person through another branch of manipulative consumerism. It happens through conversation, experience and trust.

American psychologist and one of the founders of the humanistic approach to psychology, Carl Rogers, wrote in *On Becoming a Person*: *"the more I am open to the realities in me and in the other person, the less do I find myself wishing to rush in to fix things."* Rogers was aware that people might find this approach strange because "what is life for if we are not going to teach them the things that we think they should learn?" The beauty of Rogers' answer is in its simplicity and its truth. *"The more I am simply willing to be myself, in all this complexity of life, and the more I am willing to understand and accept the realities in myself and in the other person, the more change seems to be stirred up."*

We must go back to talking face-to-face, actively listening to one another, and being present without distraction. We are desperately in need of returning to a world where it was possible for one person to feel assured by the presence of another. We have to give the present of the real world more attention. We must try not to fear what happens next, or how we appear virtually. We must spend more time in the real world.

The real world got harder to be in during the coronavirus pandemic. The move to a more digital world may well have been more in tune with how many of us live our lives, but it was also a step away from more time with other human beings. While distancing ourselves from one another to protect one another was without question the right move, the knock-on effect was a collective strain on the mental health of thousands if not millions of people. Without interaction and the presence of others, human beings are in many ways blunted instruments.

Thanks to the technology of the modern era, social connections were easier to maintain than in previous years. For that, we must be grateful, but we must also remember that nothing can replace being in a room with a friend or family member. Presence is not to be underestimated.

There is nothing wrong with wanting to grow and develop, and therefore seeing character development as an example of that, but doing it for the sake of it or in the hope of achieving something tangible, like a grade or a score, is to miss the point of it. What you get out of character development is perhaps one of the greatest parts of life. By focussing on taking the steps to understand yourself better you are developing exactly that which makes you human.

In an age where we are finally addressing mental health as a genuine illness and not something separate from the rest of the body, where the planet needs us to take greater care of it than ever before in the face of rampant expansion, where expectation on people has reached unhealthy and unrealistic levels, where children are having their youth stolen from them in exchange for an exaggerated dream that isn't anyone's to sell, it feels like the right time to pay more attention to human development.

There is much to learn from the past, but to continue to apply principles from previous eras just because they once worked or even out of fear of change is to ignore the present.

Some players already in the professional game already apply these principles themselves, independent of their clubs. Others might be very resistant to the concept. Either way, embedding it into a club is essential, not only so as to include everyone at the club but also to recognise that development of the person is intrinsically connected to development of the player.

Julie McCleery of the Center for Leadership in Athletics at the University of Washington has over 25 years of experience in youth sports education. Speaking on *The Appetite* podcast she outlined the idea of ambitious coaching, which is about recognising that aspects of development work together not as silos.

"Ambitious coaching is what happens at the intersection of peak athletic performance and social emotional growth. Successful coaches are those who pay attention to both of those things simultaneously, and who don't see them at all as mutually exclusive but see them as mutually reinforcing."

There are already many coaches doing great, balanced work. There are also clubs around the world distinctly aware of the need for this focus who have incorporated it into their philosophy. However, there is still much work to be done - particularly at the fringes of academy and first team football. Human development must not be seen as an add-on or something that happens solely as a result of the sport itself. Sport alone does not build character. Coaches need to figure out how sport can serve as a platform to aid that development. There needs to be a greater move away from the concept of "if you can't hack it, then it's not for you."

Ideally, human development is built into a club's philosophy. There will be resistance and not everyone will feel comfortable with the idea. That may change over time, but there will still be people out there who would be keen to talk about human development rather than truly implement it. The pursuit of victory and financial gain in professional sports is often to the detriment of human development. This is an opportunity to make a change, and it must be seen as well as heard.

Many people don't need to put an extra focus on it, but for all the legendary coaches in sports history who have proven it is possible to develop both the person and the player, include the community and be successful, there are others who have plenty of the skills needed to win but who might need a bit more support to make the best of their talent, and of their players' talent. Not every coach can be Bill Walsh, Bobby Robson or Jürgen Klopp, but everyone deserves a chance to take a deeper look at who they really are.

Increasing human development is to provide more and varied kinds of support in order to help as many members of the organisation. Stephen Rollnick and William Miller's aforementioned concept of Motivational Interviewing is a fantastic example of how the right kind of communication can help people find the answers they need. Much of the same emotion, with perhaps less structure, is at play in an active approach towards human development. By remembering the overarching lessons and the necessary areas of focus, it is possible to make a difference.

I think it is important in sport, particularly in football, to have more people who are invested in helping others be vulnerable, open and honest. This creates a level playing field and makes it clear that the two people are working together, not one instructing the other to go a certain way.

Despite many coaches, some of whom are in *Soul*, doing good work, the lack of development of human beings in sport environments is unsettling. Some clubs are also doing their best, but the question is not only what are we going to do about it, but also what does football, sport as a whole want to really represent?

Football's obsession with financial gain is helping too few. That greed was put into even greater focus when in April 2021, 12 European football clubs made the move to break away and form a super league. For many this was a dark day in football, albeit not an entirely unsurprising one after years of slowly inching in that direction. It was an admission from the 12 clubs in question that the communities which they represented and served were worth sacrificing for more financial gain. Business has its place in modern, professional sport, but not at this price.

Perhaps some of these forces are beyond prevention. Foreign investment may well become a norm, transfer fees may never stop growing, and financial benefits may continue to be shared among the few rather than the many. Growth and profit will reign supreme. Star power will, and perhaps in light of the super league announcement already has, become more important than location. The community will become predominantly global, digital and wired in. The local, present, founding strands between club and community won't just snap under the neglect, they will be cut. Smaller local teams may well see a surge in supporters as fans of big clubs yearn for a sport that for them is a part of their history.

And yet clubs still have a choice. Indeed, clubs have always had a choice. They can consider the entire ecosystem, the human being, personal development, the soul. A conscious choice to develop people is not anti-football, it is pro-human.

In the context of the coronavirus, the world of professional sport was largely in a privileged position. But the lengths to which football went in order to keep the show going showed a disconnect with anything to do with human development. With atmosphere literally becoming an option on your television remote, performance and results slipped into a place where they were the only things that mattered. The schedule simply reinforced the idea that all involved were machines. Games were being played in neutral venues in different countries just to make sure they were played. This was about making sure the show went on, not that those starring in it were considered. Undoubtedly, in the context of the world's suffering this plight pales, but in sport it sent a damaging message about what really mattered.

In the Disney+ production *The Mandalorian*, a fictional tale in the *Star Wars* universe about a lone bounty hunter, the central character Din Djarin lives his life according to the bounty hunter's mantra: "This is the way". The phrase is often repeated, particularly in episode three, reinforcing the idea that even a group of hired assassins in a fictional world still have a bond that unites, a phrase that both tells their history as well as their purpose.

The fictional world of Star Wars may seem like an odd place to finish, but as countless books, films, plays, songs, conversations and hopefully these chapters have shown, a story is the best format to transfer a message. Their form has changed, diversified and multiplied over the years, but we cannot escape the intrigue, adventure and emotion of a good tale. Over thousands of years, they are often the one thing endures. A good story sticks in the memory like nothing else.

Stories are intrinsically connected to human development. The values we want to encourage in others and/or help others find can be transmitted through a story and are therefore more likely to stick.

In *Mensch*, I was able to hear many stories to help me reveal what set German coaching apart. Hearing them told in person also made a great deal of difference to the understanding of the story, and this was also the case in my research and work in *Soul*. Stories can and are clearly one of the most valuable formats of communication, but actually hearing them can help with human development.

That approach might not work for some but the story has one foundational aspect that I believe can connect with everyone. Every story is written by following a framework, consciously or subconsciously. I believe parts of a framework for writing that I learned from writer, poet and friend Musa Okwonga can also be applied to helping athletes understand their role, first in football and then beyond.

When you write, it can really help to look at how, when and where you write, who you write about, what you want to say, how you will show that, how to make people care and what the journey of your story is. I think the same is true in life, including that of an athlete. Think about it.

What is your process for playing? I play outside, with friends, every day, on the training pitch, in the stadium, in front of thousands, in the afternoon, in the evening.

What is your subject? I am the subject of my story, but so is my family, my teammates, my coaches, the fans.

What do you want to say? I want to express myself through attacking football, great goals, disciplined positional play, strong tackles, aerial prowess, leading by example, assists for my teammates, winning titles for the city.

How will you show it? With commitment to my job, working hard, determined, disciplined, looking after myself, by remembering who I am playing for, by being kind, compassionate and a good teammate, by being vulnerable, by helping others and asking others for help.

How will you make people care? By showing passion and joy, by including others in my own achievements, by remembering who I am playing for, by remembering I am just one part of a team, by remembering how much people sacrifice to share these moments, by remembering the privilege that often comes with my situation.

What is the journey of your story? To remember that success comes in a variety of ways, to remember the real memories are made in the huddle not on the podium, to remember the people I played with, to remember that each step along the way rather than the finish line is really where the true joy lies, that people will remember me for who I am as much as how I play. Sami Khedira told *The Athletic* in December of 2020 as much: "Winning trophies is one thing. But when you leave, you think about the people you've met along the way, they're the ones that stick in your mind."

How we write stories is to reveal much of the structure of how we look at our lives, so perhaps returning to that framework from a sporting perspective can help the individual have a greater understanding of their own story. Even using the sporting perspective as a starting point for the answers to these questions can lead to some deeper consideration of what matters in life and how much of that is not about what happens on the field or the court.

There is great value in having purpose, perhaps even more in just considering it. However, as the powerful and emotional Pixar movie *Soul* showed, we must not forget that life is in fact all of the other bits along the way. Joe's realisation that his dream of "making it" as a jazz musician blinded him from seeing all of the magical moments in his life. What we do or what we achieve should not be the sole purpose of our life. This is no different for all those hoping to make it in professional sport. And both those who do make the transition to the professional arena as well as those who do not need support to remember that life is not about whether you played in the Premier League or not. Life is so much more. As hard as it is for human beings to do so in a world that so often demands and drains, we must try to look at how it also delivers - every day.

In *The Mandalorian*, the message is about a way of life being integral to the preservation of the bounty hunters' existence. In football, as in many careers, a future consisting of healthy humans is only possible if we nurture the person - and the planet. For too long we have told ourselves the story we want to hear rather than the one which truly reflects what is happening. There are many great people out there doing their best to care for and help develop human beings, but they are too few and too unsupported by the structure within which they work.

It is time to change that. American anthropologist David Graeber once wrote in *The Utopia of Rules: On Technology, Stupidity, and the Secret Joys of Bureaucracy* that *"the ultimate, hidden truth of the world is that it is something that we make, and could just as easily make differently."*

The world is not a set form. One look at the deforestation of the planet in order to sustain the world's rampant growth shows as much, but the same is true of structures, cultures and societies. These are not set forms. They can be changed. In many respects, we will need more than self-belief to get there. Luck, support and help from those more privileged than us will likely play key roles. But it is possible.

I believe the same is true for looking after the person in sport. It is possible to care for the person and still win. What is sport without the person, the community or everyday interactions? Indeed, what is life without all of that?

There is not one definitive way to put human beings first, there are many. The key is deciding to do it, recognising that if the soul burns brightly then much more can too. Looking after the human being is the way. Now sport must choose it. It must choose soul.

Acknowledgements

A huge thank you to everyone I spoke to for this book. Without their work and insights, the exploration into the premise of this book would not have been possible. Thanks to Frederik Bløndal, Piotr Haren, Tom Vernon, Dr. Carsten Hvid Larsen, Will Orben, James C. Nortey, James Vaughan, Dennis Hörtin, Mark O'Sullivan, Scott Swainston, Dr. Richard Bailey, the academy coach in Germany, Simon Williams, Tim Sparv, Dr. Wade Gilbert, Nick Cox, Stephen Rollnick, Dr. Suzanne Brown, Rick Cotgreave, Hugo Scheckter, Steve Johnson, Paul Heptonstall, Nils Nielsen, Nora Häuptle, Chris Rush, Tom Dent, Bjørn Mannsverk, Ben Freakley, Jordan Ferrell, Lisa Bonta Sumii, Chris Ramsey, Marvin Sordell - I am grateful not only for the time you gave me and what I learned from you but also for the work you do.

Huge thanks must also go to Ian Hunter for his help with all of the baseball part of this book. I could not have completed the work on the Blue Jays without his help and guidance when it came to America's most traditional game.

I would like to thank Musa, Jenn and Ryan for their constant belief and inspiration, Ali and Sophie for their friendship and knowledge, and the Sanders family for all the joint adventures.

I owe so much to my publisher David Hartrick. I am grateful for your belief and the continued opportunity to do this work this way. Thank you. A huge thank you also to Steve Hill for his help editing and Mick Kinlan for another great cover design.

Thanks to both of my families for all their love and support over the years, and all they've done to help me as a boy and later as a man. Thanks to my brother, Matthew, for sparking so many ideas, to my Dad for all the faith, and my Mum for giving me the platform in life to be a good man. I love you all so much.

Dan, thanks for being the best friend ever and for teaching me so much about life and emotion. I would not be the man I am without you and your friendship. Elizabeth, I am so lucky to know you and

I love you and Danny so much.

To everyone who read *Mensch*, thank you. I wrote that book to elevate the voices of German coaches but also in the hope those tales would resonate with others. I am so grateful for the feedback. It has been overwhelming. I hope *Soul* was equally worth your time. Thank you for choosing to read it.

Thanks to the following:

Websites:
- The American Foundation for the Blind
- SportBladet
- Gapminder
- Esquire
- The Guardian
- Sports Illustrated
- The Talent Equation
- news.com.au
- The Athletic
- Forbes
- Anxiety and Depression Association of America
- The Nation
- Cleveland Magazine
- BBC Sport
- The Coaches' Voice
- Harvard Business Review
- Wisden Cricket Monthly
- Cano Football
- NBC Sports
- ERI - Economic Research Institute

Podcasts:
- Rasenfunk
- Don't Tell Me The Score
- The Michelle Obama Podcast
- Beyond The Grid
- Learning in Development
- The Appetite
- How to Save a Planet
- Football Ramble

Books:

- Factfulness - Hans Rosling, Ola Rosling, Anna Rolsing Rönnlund
- Notes on a Nervous Planet - Matt Haig
- Emotional Intelligence: Why it can matter more than IQ - Daniel Goleman
- The Chimp Paradox - Dr. Steve Peters
- Good to Great - Jim Collins
- Motivational Interviewing: Helping people to change - William Miller & Stephen Rollnick
- The Road to Character - David Brooks
- On Becoming a Person - Carl Rogers
- Gwynne's Grammar - N. M. Gwynne
- The Utopia of Rules: On Technology, Stupidity, and the Secret Joys of Bureaucracy - David Graeber
- Individual Psychotherapy and the Science of Psychodynamics, 2Ed - David Malan
- The Captain Class - Sam Walker
- No Hunger in Paradise - Michael Calvin
- The Open Door - Helen Keller

TV/Film:

- The Last Dance
- Luc Longley and the 'missing chapter' of the Last Dance
- TEDx
- The Mandalorian
- Soul

Journals:

- *Noora J. Ronkainen, Kenneth Aggerholm, Tatiana V. Ryba & Jacquelyn Allen-Collinson (2020): Learning in sport: from life skills to existential learning, Sport, Education and Society, DOI: 10.1080/13573322.2020.1712655*
- *Curran, T., & Hill, A. P. (2019). Perfectionism is increasing over time: A meta-analysis of birth co-hort differences from 1989 to 2016. Psychological Bulletin, 145(4), 410–429.*
- *Vaughan James, Mallett Clifford J., Davids Keith, Potrac Paul, López-Felip Maurici A. (2019): Developing Creativity to Enhance Human Potential in Sport: A Wicked Transdisciplinary Challenge: Frontiers in Psychology: DOI:*

10.3389/fpsyg.2019.02090: ISSN=1664-1078

- *Poli Roberto. (2013): A Note on the Difference Between Complicated and Complex Social Systems: CADMUS, Volume 2, No.1, October 2013, 142-147*
- *Bergeron MF, Mountjoy M, Armstrong N (2015), et al International Olympic Committee consen-sus statement on youth athletic development, British Journal of Sports Medicine;49:843-851*
- *Andrew Kirkland and Mark O'Sullivan (2018), There Is No Such Thing as an International Elite Under-9 Soccer Player, J Sports Sci Med. 2018 Dec; 17(4): 686–688. Published online 2018 Nov 20. PMCID: PMC6243622 PMID: 30479539*
- *McCready, C (2019) And vs Or: Apprentice footballers' understanding of identity and personal development. Doctoral thesis, Liverpool John Moores University. 10.24377/LJMU.t.00011959*
- *Alvarez Zamora, A. (2011), Professional football players and labor market insertion strategies af-ter withdrawal. AGON International Journal of Sport Sciences 1(2), 115-128.*
- *Richard Elliott (2020): The man who would be worth billions: Vincent Pericard, migration and mental illness, European Journal for Sport and Society, DOI: 10.1080/16138171.2020.1823690*
- *Nicola A. Sothern & Jimmy O'Gorman (2021): Exploring the mental health and wellbeing of pro-fessional academy footballers in England, Soccer & Society, DOI: 10.1080/14660970.2021.1952693*
- *Sherman LE, Payton AA, Hernandez LM, Greenfield PM, Dapretto M. The Power of the Like in Adolescence: Effects of Peer Influence on Neural and Behavioral Responses to Social Media. Psychological Science. 2016;27(7):1027-1035. doi:10.1177/0956797616645673*